Miss.] [Coulton

Our farm of four acres

and the money we made by it

Miss.] [Coulton

Our farm of four acres
and the money we made by it

ISBN/EAN: 9783744739887

Printed in Europe, USA, Canada, Australia, Japan

Cover: Foto ©ninafisch / pixelio.de

More available books at **www.hansebooks.com**

OUR FARM OF FOUR ACRES

AND

THE MONEY WE MADE BY IT.

From the Twelfth London Edition.

WITH AN INTRODUCTION
BY PETER B. MEAD,
EDITOR OF THE HORTICULTURIST.

NEW YORK:
C. M. SAXTON, BARKER & COMPANY,
NO. 25 PARK ROW.
1860.

Preface to the Twelfth London Edition.

This little volume has been received with so much favor, both by the public and the press, that I cannot refrain from expressing my gratitude for the kind treatment I have experienced. From many of the criticisms which have appeared respecting "Our Farm of Four Acres," I have received not only complimentary remarks, but likewise some useful hints on the subjects of which I have written. With the praise comes some little censure; and I am charged by more than one friendly critic with stupidity for not ordering the legs of our first cow to be strapped, which would, they consider, have prevented both milk and milker from being knocked over. Now this was done, but the animal had a way of knocking the man and pail down with her side; every means was tried, but nothing succeeded till her calf was parted with. We have been asked whether we had to keep gates, hedges, &c., in repair, or whether it was done at the expense of the landlord. As far as regarded the gates and buildings, that gentleman was bound by agreement to keep them in order, and as for hedges we have none. A stream runs round the meadows, and forms the boundary of our small domain. Since our little work was written we have had nearly eighteen months' further experience, and have as much reason now as then to be satisfied with the profits we receive from our four acres. I must add a few words concerning our butter-making. Some doubts have been expressed relative to our power of churning for four hours at a time. Now it certainly was not pleasant, but it was not the hard work that some people imagine: fatiguing certainly; but then H. and myself took it, as children say, "turn and turn about." We did not entrust the churn to Tom, because he was liable to be called away to perform some of his many duties. Had we not had the toil, we should not have acquired the knowledge which now enables us to complete our work in three-quarters of an hour. We have been pitied for being always employed, and told that we can never know the luxury of leisure. We answer this remark with the words of "Poor Richard," that "leisure is the time for doing something useful."

INTRODUCTION

TO THE AMERICAN EDITION.

This little volume will possess rare interest for all who own a " four-acre farm," or, indeed, a farm of any number of acres. Its chief value to the American reader does not consist in its details of practice, but in the enunciation and demonstration of certain principles of domestic economy of universal application. The practice of terra-culture must be varied to meet the different conditions of soil and climate under which it is pursued ; but sound general principles hold good everywhere, and only need the exercise of ordinary judgment and common sense for their application to our own wants. This is now better understood than heretofore, and hence we are better prepared to profit by draughts from the fount of universal knowledge. We would not be understood as intimating, however, that only the general principles set forth in this little book are of value to us ; the details of making butter and bread, feeding stock, etc., are just as useful to us as to the English reader. The two chapters on making butter and bread are admirable in their way, and alone are worth the price of the book. So, too, of domestics and their management; we have to go through pretty much the same vexations, probably a little intensified, as there is among us a more rampant spirit of independence on the part of servants; but many of these vexations may be avoided, we have no doubt, by following the suggestion of our author, of procuring "country help" for the country. Domestics accustomed to city life not only lack the requisite knowledge, but are unwilling to learn, and will not readily adapt themselves to the circumstances in which they are placed; in fact, the majority of them "know too much," and are altogether too impatient of control. A woman, however, must be mistress in her own house; this is indispensable to economy and comfort; and the plan adopted by our author will often secure this when all others fail.

We have not deemed it advisable to add anything in the way of notes; we have made a few alterations in the text to adapt it better to the wants of the American reader, and for the same reason we have altered the English currency to our own. In other respects the work remains intact. In some works of this kind notes would have been indispensable, but in the present case we have thought we could safely trust to the judgment of the reader to appropriate and adapt the general principles set forth, leaving the application of details to the shrewdness and strong common sense characteristic of the American mind. The object of the work is rather to demonstrate a general principle than to furnish all the minutiæ of practice, though enough of these are given to serve the purpose of illustration. The American reader will not fail, of course, to make due allowance for the difference of rent, prices, etc., between this country and England, and the matter of adaptation then becomes a very simple affair.

In conclusion, we present the work as a model in style. It is written with a degree of simplicity which makes it readily understood, and is a fine specimen of good old Anglo-Saxon. Portions of it are fully as interesting as a romance. It is written by a lady, which fact gives it an additional interest and value as a contribution to the economy of country life, in which it may be admitted that women are our masters. The incidents connected with hiring "our farm of four acres" are related in a life-like manner, and will be appreciated by our own May-day hunting countrywomen, who, we trust, will also appreciate the many important facts set forth in this little volume, which we heartily commend to them and to all others, with the wish that it may be as useful and popular here as it has been at home. P. B. M.

CONTENTS.

CHAP.	PAGE
I.—WHERE SHALL WE LIVE?	7
II.—OUR FIRST DIFFICULTY	21
III.—OUR SECOND COW	29
IV.—HOW TO MAKE BUTTER	36
V.—WHAT WE MADE BY OUR COWS	41
VI.—OUR PIGS	45
VII.—OUR POULTRY	51
VIII.—OUR LOSSES	56
IX.—OUR PIGEONS	61
X.—HOW WE CURED OUR HAMS	67
XI.—OUR BREAD	72
XII.—OUR KITCHEN-GARDEN	79
XIII.—THE MONEY WE MADE	88
XIV.—THE NEXT SIX MONTHS	94
XV.—OUR PONY	113
XVI.—CONCLUSION	120

OUR FARM OF FOUR ACRES.

CHAPTER I.

WHERE SHALL WE LIVE?

"WHERE shall we live?" That was a question asked by the sister of the writer, when it became necessary to leave London, and break up a once happy home, rendered desolate by sudden bereavement.

"Ah! where, indeed?" was the answer. "Where can we hope to find a house which will be suitable for ourselves, six children, and a small income?"

"Oh," answered H., "there can be no difficulty about that. Send for the 'Times' and we shall find dozens of places that will do for us." So that mighty organ of information was procured, and its columns eagerly searched.

"But," said I, "what sort of place do we really mean to take?"

"That," replied H., "is soon settled. We must have

a good-sized dining-room, small drawing-room, and a breakfast-room, which may be converted into a school-room. It must have a nursery and five good bed-chambers, a chaise-house, and stable for the pony and carriage, a large garden, and three or four acres of land, for we must keep a cow. It must not be more than eight miles from 'town,' or two from a station; it must be in a good neighborhood, and it must——"

"Stop! stop!" cried I; "how much do you intend to give a-year for all these conveniences?"

"How much? Why, I should say we ought not to give more than $250."

"We *ought* not," said I, gravely, "but I greatly fear we shall for that amount have to put up with a far inferior home to the one you contemplate. But come, let us answer a few of these advertisements; some of them depict the very place you wish for."

So after selecting those which, when they had described in bright colors the houses to be let, added, "Terms very moderate," we "presented compliments" to Messrs. A., B., C., D., and in due time received cards to view the "desirable country residences" we had written about. But our hopes of becoming the fortunate occupants of any one of those charming abodes were soon dashed to the ground; for with the cards came the terms; and we found that a "very moderate rental" meant from $600 to $750 per annum. We looked at each other rather ruefully; and the ungenerous remark of "I told you so" rose to my lips. However, I did not give it utterance, but substituted the words, "Never mind, let us send for another 'Times,' and only answer those advertisements which state plainly the rent required." This time we enlarged our ideas on the subjects of rent and distance, and resolved that if that beautiful place *near* Esher would suit us, we would not mind giving $300 a-year for it.

In a few days arrived answers to our last inquiries. We fixed on the one which appeared the most eligible, but were a little dismayed to find that "near Esher" meant six miles from the station.

"Never mind," said H., resolutely, "the pony can take us to it in fine weather, and in winter we must not want to go to London.

We started the next morning by rail, and found the "Cottage" almost as pretty as it had appeared on paper. But, alas! it had been let the day previous to our arrival, and we had to return to town minus five dollars for our expenses.

The next day, nothing daunted,—indeed, rather encouraged by finding the house we had seen really equal to our expectations,—we set off to view another "villa," which, from the particulars we had received from the agent, appeared quite as attractive. This time we found the place tenantless; and, as far as we were concerned, it would certainly remain so. It had been represented as a "highly-desirable country residence, and quite ready for the reception of a family of respectability." It was dignified with the appellation of Middlesex Hall," and we were rather surprised when we found that this high-sounding name signified a mean-looking place close to the road; and when the door was opened for our admission, that we stepped at once from the small front court into the drawing-room, from which a door opened into a stone kitchen. The rest of the accommodation corresponded with this primitive mode of entrance; the whole place was in what is commonly called a "tumble-down" condition: there was certainly plenty of garden, and two large meadows, but, like the rest of the place, they were sadly out of order. When we said it was not at all the house we had expected to find from reading the advertisement, we were asked what sort of house we expected to get for $300 with five acres of land. Now that was a question we could not have answered had we not seen the pretty cottage with nearly as much ground at Esher; however, we did not give the owner the benefit of our experience, but merely said that the house would not suit us, and drove back four miles to the station, rather out of spirits with the result of our day's work.

For more than a fortnight did we daily set forth on this voyage of discovery. One day we started with a card to view "a delightful Cottage Ornée, situated four miles from Weybridge;" this time the rent was still higher than any we had previously seen. When we arrived at the village in which the house was represented to be, we asked for "Heathfield House," and were told that no one knew of any residence bearing that name; we were a little perplexed, and consulted the card of admittance to see whether we had brought the wrong one—but no; there it was, "Heathfield

House," four miles from Weybridge, surrounded by its own grounds of four acres, tastefully laid out in lawn, flower and kitchen-gardens, &c., &c. Rent only $350. We began to imagine that we were the victims of some hoax, and were just on the point of telling the driver to return to the station, when a dirty-looking man came to the carriage, and said, " Are you looking for Heathfield House ?"

" Yes," said we.

" Well, I'll show it to you."

" Is it far ?" we asked ; as no sign of a decent habitation was to be seen near us.

" No ; just over the way," was the answer.

We looked in the direction he indicated, and saw a " brick carcase " standing on a bare, heathy piece of ground, without enclosure of any kind.

" That !" cried we ; " it is impossible that can be the place we came to see !"

" Have you got a card from Mr. —— ?" was the query addressed to us.

" Yes," was the reply.

" Very well ; then if you will get out I'll show it to you."

As we had come so far we thought we might as well finish the adventure, and accordingly followed our guide over the piece of rough muddy ground which led to the brick walls before us. We found them on a nearer inspection quite as empty as they appeared from the road; neither doors nor windows were placed in them, and the staircases were not properly fixed. It was with much trouble we succeeded in reaching the floor where the bed-chambers were to be, and found that not even the boards were laid down. We told our conductor that the place would not suit us, as we were compelled to remove from our present residence in three weeks.

"Well, if that's all that hinders your taking it, I'll engage to get it all ready in that time."

"What! get the staircases fixed, the doors and windows put in, the walls papered and painted?"

"Yes," was answered, in a confident tone, which expressed indignation at the doubt we had implied.

We then ventured to say, that, "Allowing he could get the house ready by the time we required to move, we saw no sign of the coach-house and stable, lawn or flower-garden, kitchen-garden or meadow."

"As for the coach-house and stable," said the showman, "I can get your horses put up in the village."

We hastened to disclaim the *horses,* and humbly confessed that our stud consisted of one pony only.

"The less reason to be in a hurry for the stable, for you can put one pony anywhere; and as for the lawn and gardens, they will be laid out when the house is let; and the heath will be levelled and sown for a meadow, and anything else done for a good tenant that is in reason."

We were likewise assured that wonders had been done already, for that four months ago the ground was covered with furze. We got rid of our talkative friend with the promise that we would "think of it;" and, indeed, we *did* think, that Mr. ——, who was a very respectable house-agent, ought to ascertain what sort of places were placed in his hands before he sent people on such profitless journeys. The expense attending this one amounted to nearly eight dollars.

Another week was passed in a similar manner, in going distances varying from ten to twenty-five miles daily in pursuit of houses which we were induced to think must suit us, but when seen proved as deceptive as those I have mentioned. We gained nothing by our travels but the loss of time, money, and hope. At last the idea entered our heads of going to some of the house-agents, and looking over their books.

Our first essay was at the office of Mr. A. B., in Bond street. "Have you any houses to let at such a distance from town, with such a quantity of land, such a number of rooms?" &c.

"Oh, yes, madam," said the smiling clerk, and immediately opened a large ledger; "what rent do you propose giving?"

"From $250 to $350 yearly," answered we, and felt how respectable we must appear in the opinion of the smart gentleman whom we addressed; how great then was our surprise when he closed his large volume with a crash, and with a look of supreme contempt said, "*We* have nothing of that kind in *our* books." To use one of Fanny Kemble's expressions, "we felt mean," and left the office of this aristocratical house-agent half ashamed of our humble fortunes.

I fear I should tire the patience of the reader, did I detail all our "adventures in search of a house," but we must entreat indulgence for our last journey. We once more started on the South-Western line, to see a house which, from the assurances we had received from the owner, resident in London, must at last be *the* house, and for which the rent asked was $350; but once more were we doomed to disappointment by finding that the "handsome dining and drawing-rooms" were two small parlors, with doors opening into each other; and that "five excellent bed-chambers" were three small rooms and two wretched attics.

From the station to this place was four miles; and, as weary and hopeless we were returning to it, it occurred to H. to ask the driver if he knew of any houses to let in the vicinity. He considered, and then said he only knew of one, which had been vacant some time, and that parties who had been to see it would not take it because it was situated in a bad neighborhood.

At the commencement of our search that would have been quite sufficient to have deterred us from looking at it, but we could not now afford to be fastidious. Our own house was let, and move from it we must in less than a fortnight; so we desired the driver to take us into this bad neighborhood, and were rewarded for the additional distance we travelled by finding an old-fashioned, but very convenient house, with plenty of good-sized rooms in excellent repair, a very pretty flower-garden, with greenhouse, good kitchen-garden of one acre, an orchard of the same extent well stocked with fine fruit-trees, three acres of good meadow-land, an excellent coach-house and stabling, with houses for cows, pigs, and poultry, all in good order.

The "bad neighborhood" was not so very bad. The cottages just outside the gates were small, new buildings; and once inside, you saw nothing but your own grounds. It possessed the advantage of being less than two miles from a station, and not more than twelve from London.

"This will do," we both exclaimed, "if the rent is not too high."

We had been asked $600 for much inferior places; so that it was with great anxiety we directed our civil driver to take us to the party who had the disposal of the house. When there, we met with the welcome intelligence, that house, gardens, orchard, meadows, and buildings, were all included in a rental of $370 per annum. We concluded the bargain there and then, and on that day fortnight took possession of " Our Farm of Four Acres."

Before we close this chapter, we will address a few words to such of our readers as may entertain the idea that houses in the country may be had " for next to nothing." We had repeatedly heard this asserted, and when we resolved to give $300 a year, we thought that we should have no difficulty in meeting with a respectable habitation for that sum, large enough for our family and with the quantity of land we required, as well as within a moderate distance of London. We have already told the reader how fallacious we found this hope to be. Houses within forty or fifty miles of London, in what are called " good situations," are nearly, if not quite as high rented, as those in the suburbs, and land worth quite as much. If at any time a "cheap place" is to be met with, be quite sure that there is some drawback to compensate for the low price.

In our pilgrimages to empty houses, we frequently found some which were low-rented, that is, from $200 to $250 per annum ; but either they were much smaller than we required, or dreadfully out of repair, or else they were built "Cockney fashion," semi-detached, or, as was frequently the case, situated in a locality which for some reason or other was highly objectionable. We always found rents lower in proportion to the distance from a station.

We one day went to Beaconsfield to view a house, and had a fly from Slough, a drive of several miles. The house was in the middle of the town, large and convenient, with good garden and paddock; the whole was offered us for $200 yearly; and we should have taken it, had it not been in such a dismantled condition that the agent in whose hands it was placed informed us that though he had orders to put it in complete repair, he would not promise it would be fit for occupation under several months. The office of this gentleman was next door to Mr. A. B.'s, in Bond street; and we are bound to state, that though we said that we did not wish to give more than $300, we were treated with respect; and several offered us under these terms, though attended with circumstances which prevented our availing ourselves of them.

The house we at last found was not, as regarded situation, what we liked; not because of the cottages close to the entrance, but for the reason that there was no "view," but from the top windows; as far as the lower part of the house was concerned, we might as well have been in the Clapham Road. It is true we looked into gardens, front and back, but that was all; and we had to go through two or three streets of the little town in which we were located whenever we left the house for a walk. Still we were, on the whole, well pleased with our new home, and in the next chapter will tell the reader how we commenced a life so different to that we had been accustomed to lead.

CHAPTER II.

OUR FIRST DIFFICULTY.

ONCE fairly settled in our new habitation, and all the important affairs attending the necessary alterations of carpets, curtains, etc., being nearly finished, we began to wonder what we were to do with "Our Farm of Four Acres." That we must keep a cow was acknowledged by both; and the first step to be taken was to buy one. The small town in which our house was situated boasted of a market weekly, and there we resolved to make the important purchase. Accordingly, we sent our man-of-all-work to inspect those offered for sale. Shortly he returned, accompanied by a small black cow, with a calf a week old. We purchased these animals for $50; and it was very amusing to see all the half-dozen children running into the stable-yard, with their little cups, to enjoy the first-fruits of their country life. But what proved far more of a treat than the new milk was the trouble of procuring it, for the cow proved a very spiteful one, and knocked the unfortunate milker, with his pail, "heels-over-head." As he was not in the least hurt, the juveniles were allowed to laugh as long as they pleased; but H. and myself looked rather grave at the idea of having the milk knocked down as soon as there was about a quart in the pail. We were, therefore, greatly reässured when told that "Madam Sukey" would be quiet and tractable as soon as her calf was taken away. "Then why not take it at once?" said I; but was informed that we must not deprive her of it for a week. However, I am bound to confess that our first week's farming turned out badly, for the cow would not be milked, quietly, and every morning we were informed that two men were obliged to be called in to hold her while she was milked. At the end of the week we sold the calf for five dollars, and after a month the cow became on quite friendly terms with her milker, and has proved ever since very profitable to our small dairy.

We did not contemplate making butter with one cow, as we thought so large a household would consume all the milk. Very soon, however, "nurse" complained that "the milk was 'too rich' for the children; it was not in the least like London milk; it must either be watered or skimmed for the little ones: but she would rather have it skimmed." That was done, and for a whole fortnight H. and myself used nothing but cream in our tea and coffee. At first this was a great luxury, and we said continually to each other, how delightful it was to have such a dainty in profusion. Soon, like the children, we began to discover it was "too good for us," and found that we liked plenty of new milk much better for general use; besides, consume as much as we would, we had still more than was wanted: so we invested fifteen dollars in a churn and other requisites, and thought with great satisfaction of the saving we should effect in our expenses by making our own butter. But now arose a difficulty which had not previously occurred to us: Who was to make it? Our domestic servants both declared that they could not do so; and the elder one, who had been many years in the family, was born and bred in London, and detested the country and everything connected with it, gave her opinion in the most decided manner, that there was quite enough "muck" in the house already, without making more work with butter-making, which, she said confidently, would only be fit for the pig when it was made. Here was a pretty state of things! what were we to do? must we give up all hope of eating our own butter, and regard the money as lost which we had just expended for the churn, etc.? After a few minutes' bewilderment, the idea occurred to both of us at the same moment: " Cannot we make the butter, and be independent of these household rebels?"

"But," said I, dolefully, "we don't in the least know how to set about it."

"What of that?" replied H.: "where was the use of expending so much money in books relative to a country life as you did before we left town, if they are not to enlighten our ignorance on country matters? But one thing is certain, we cannot make butter till we have learnt *how;* so let us endeavor to obtain the requisite knowledge to do so to-morrow."

We accordingly devoted the remainder of the day to consulting the various books on domestic and rural economy we had collected together previous to leaving London. Greatly puzzled we were by them. On referring to the subject of butter-making, one authority said, "you must never wash the butter, but only knock it on a board, in order to get the buttermilk from it." Another only told us to "well cleanse the buttermilk from it," without giving us an idea how the process was to be accomplished; while the far-famed Mrs. Rundle, in an article headed "Dairy," tells the dairy-maid to "keep a book in which to enter the amount of butter she makes," and gives but little idea how the said butter is to be procured. Another authority said, "after the butter is come, cut it in pieces to take out the cow-hairs;" this appeared to us the oddest direction of all, for surely it was possible to remove them from the cream before it was put into the churn. We were very much dissatisfied with the amount of practical knowledge we gleaned from our books; they seemed to us written for the benefit of those who already were well acquainted with the management of a dairy, and consequently of very little service to those who wished to acquire the rudiments of the art of butter-making.

The next morning we proceeded to make a trial, and the first thing we did was to strain the cream through a loose fine cloth into the churn, then taking the handle we began to turn it vigorously;* the weather was hot, and after churning for more than an hour, there seemed as little prospect of butter as when we commenced. We stared at each other in blank amazement. Must we give it up? No; that was not to be thought of. H. suddenly remembered, that somewhere she had heard that in warm weather you should put the churn in cold water. As ours was a box one, we did not see how we could manage this; but the bright idea entered her head, that if we could not put the water outside the churn we might *in:* so we pumped a quart of spring-water into it and churned away with fresh hopes: nor were we disappointed; in about a quarter of an hour we heard quite a different sound as we turned the handle, which assured us that the cream had undergone a change, and taking off the lid—(how many times had we taken it off before!)—we saw what at that moment appeared the most welcome sight in the world—some lumps of rich yellow butter. It was but a small quantity, but there it was: the difficulty

---

* Ninety times in a minute is the proper speed with which the handle should be turned.

was overcome so far. But now there arose the question of what we were to do with it in order to clean it from the butter milk, for all our authorities insisted on the necessity of this being done, though they did not agree in the mode of doing it. One said, that "if it was washed, it would not keep good, because water soon became putrid, and so would the butter." We were told by another book, "that if it was *not* washed it would be of two colors, and dreadfully rank." We thought that it would be easier not to wash it, and it was bad enough to justify the term "*muck*," which was applied to it by the kitchen oracles, who rejoiced exceedingly in our discomfiture. We left the dairy half inclined to abjure butter-making for the future. In a day or two we began to reflect, that as we had a "Farm of Four Acres," we must manage to do something with it, and what so profitable to a large family as making butter? So, when we had collected sufficient cream, we tried again, and this time with great success. We commenced as before, by straining the cream, and then taking the handle of the churn we turned it more equally than we had done before; in half an hour we heard the welcome sound which proclaimed that the "butter was come." This time we washed it well; it was placed in a pan under the pump, and the water suffered to run on it till not the least milkiness appeared in it; we then removed it to a board that had been soaking for some time in cold water, salted it to our taste, and afterwards, with two flat boards, such as butter-men use in London shops, made it up into rolls. It was as good as it could be, and we were delighted to think that we had conquered all the difficulties attending its manufacture: but we had yet to discover the truth of the proverb, that "one swallow does not make a summer."

CHAPTER III.

OUR SECOND COW.

WE soon found that we could not expect to supply our family with butter from one cow, and we thought that, as we had to perform the duties of dairy-women, we might as well have the full benefit of our labor. We, therefore, purchased another cow; but before doing so, were advised not this time to have a Welsh one, but to give more money and have a larger animal. This we did, and bought a very handsome strawberry-colored one, for which, with the calf, we gave $75; and here it will be as well to say that we think it was $25 thrown away, for in no respect did she prove more valuable than the black one, for which we had given but $50. For a small dairy, we think the black Welsh cow answers as well, or better, than any other. The price is very small, and, judging from our own, they are very profitable. They are also much hardier than those of a larger breed, and may be kept out all the winter, excepting when snow is on the ground.

After our new cow had been in our possession just a week, we received one morning the unwelcome intelligence that the "new cow" was very bad. We went into the meadow, and saw the poor creature looking certainly as we had been told, "very bad." We asked our factotum what was the matter with her. To this he replied, that he did not know, but that he had sent for a man who was "very clever in cows."

In a short time this clever man arrived, bringing with him a friend, likewise learned in cattle. He went to see the patient, and returned to us looking very profound.

"A bad job!" said he, with a shake of the head worthy of Sheridan's Lord Burleigh. "A sad job, indeed! and you only bought her last market-day. Well, it can't be helped."

"But what ails her?" said I.

"What ails her! why, she's got the lung disease."

"But what is that?" said I.

"What's that! why, it's what kills lots of cows; takes 'em off in two or three days. You must sell her for what she'll fetch. Perhaps you may get $10 for her. I'll get rid of her for you."

"But," said H., "if she has the 'lung disease' you talk of, you tell us she must die."

"Yes; she'll die, sure enough."

"Well, then, who will buy a cow that is sure to be dead to-morrow or next day?"

"Oh, that's no concern of yours! *You* get rid of her, that's all."

To this dictum we rather demurred, and resolved to send for a cow-doctor, and see if she could be cured; if not, to take care she was not converted after her death into "country sausages," for the benefit of London consumers of those dainties. Our friendly counsellor was very indignant at our perversity in not getting rid of a cow with "the lung disease," and stumped out of the yard in a fit of virtuous indignation. With proper treatment the cow soon got well.

We still had occasional trouble with our butter-making; sometimes it would come in half an hour, sometimes we were hard at work with the churn for two or three hours, and then the butter was invariably bad. We tried to procure information on the subject, and asked several farmers' wives in the neighborhood "how long butter ought to be in coming." We always received the same answer :—

"Why, you see, ma'am, that depends."

"Well," we asked, "what does it depend on?"

"Oh, on lots of things."

"Well, tell us some of the things on which it depends."

"Why, you see it's longer coming in hot weather, and it's longer coming in cold weather; and it depends on how long the cow has calved, and how you churn, and on lots beside."

We found we must endeavor to discover for ourselves the reason why we were half an hour in getting it one day, and the next, perhaps, two or three hours.

As the weather became colder we found it more troublesome, and one frosty day we churned four hours without success. We put in cold water, we put in hot, we put in salt, we talked of adding vinegar, but did not; we churned as fast as we could turn the handle, and then as slowly as possible, but still no butter. At the end of more than four hours our labors were rewarded. The butter came; strong, rank stuff it was.

We determined before the next churning day to try and find out the reason of all this trouble. We once more took to our books, but were none the wiser, for none of them told us anything about the particular thing we searched for. After many experiments we tried the effect of bringing the cream into the kitchen over night, and see if warmth would make any difference. It was guess-work for two or three churnings, but the discovery was made at last, that we were always sure of our butter in half an hour, provided the cream was, when put into the churn, at a temperature of from 50° to 60°.* No matter how long the cow had calved, how hot or how cold the weather, if we put the cream into the churn at that degree of heat the butter was sure to come, in as near as possible the time we have specified.

This, in the winter, was effected by bringing the cream-pot into the kitchen over night, and if the

---

* We kept a small thermometer for the purpose of plunging into the cream-pot. If it was lower than 55° we waited till it reached that degree: if the weather was very warm, and it rose higher than we have specified, we did not attempt to churn till by some means we had lowered it to the proper temperature.

weather was very cold, placing it on a chair a moderate distance from the fire for about a quarter of an hour in the morning : boiling water was likewise put into the churn for half an hour before it was used.

Now, no doubt, a regular dairymaid would "turn up her nose" at all these details.; but I do not write for those who know their business, but for the benefit of those ladies who, as is now so much the custom, reside a few miles from the city or town in which the business or profession of their husbands may be situated. In many cases they take with them town-bred servants to a country residence; and then, like ourselves, find they know nothing whatever of the duties required of them. To those who have several acres of pasture land, of course this little book is all "bosh." They employ servants who know their work and perform it properly; but most "suburbans" require the cook to undertake the duties of the dairy, and unless they are regular country servants they neither do their work well nor willingly. If any lady who has one or two cows will instruct her servant to follow our directions, she will always be sure of good butter, with very little trouble. All that is required is a churn, milk-pans (at the rate of three to each cow), a milk-pail, a board (or, better still, a piece of marble), to make the butter up on, a couple of butter-boards, such as are used in the shops to roll it into form, and a crock for the cream.

In the next chapter we will give, as concisely as we can, the whole process that we ourselves used in our dairy.

CHAPTER IV.

HOW TO MAKE BUTTER.

LET the cream be at the temperature of 55° to 60°; if the weather is cold, put boiling water into the churn for half an hour before you want to use it: when that is poured off, strain in the cream through a butter-cloth. When the butter is coming, which is easily ascertained by the sound, take off the lid, and with one of the flat boards scrape down the sides of the churn; and do the same to the lid: this prevents waste. When the butter is come, the buttermilk is to be poured off and spring-water put in the churn, and turned for two or three minutes: this is to be then poured away, and fresh added, and again the handle turned for a minute or two. Should there be the least appearance of milkiness when this is poured from the churn, more is to be put. This we found was a much better mode of extracting all the buttermilk than placing it in a pan under the pump, as we did when we commenced our labors. The butter is then to be placed on the board or marble, and salted to taste; then, with a cream-cloth, wrung out of spring-water, press all the moisture from it. When it appears quite dry and firm, make it up into rolls with the flat boards. The whole process should be completed in three-quarters of an hour.

We always used a large tub which was made for the purpose, and every article we were going to use was soaked in it for half an hour in boiling water; then that removed, and cold spring-water substituted; and the things we required remained in it till they were wanted. This prevents the butter from adhering to the boards, cloth, &c., which would render the task of "making it up" both difficult and disagreeable.

In hot weather, instead of bringing the cream-crock into the kitchen it must be kept as cool as possible; for as it is essential in the winter to raise the temperature of the cream to the degree I have stated, so in the summer it must be lowered to it. Should your dairy not be cool enough for the purpose, it is best effected by keeping the cream-pot in water as cold as you can procure it, and by making the butter early in the morning, and placing cold water in the churn some time before it is used. By following these directions you will have good butter throughout the year.

The cows should be milked as near the dairy as possible, as it prevents the cream from rising well if the milk is carried any distance.* It should be at once strained into the milk-pans, and not disturbed for forty-eight hours in winter, and twenty-four in summer. In hot weather it is highly important that the cream should be perfectly strained from the milk, or it will make it very rank. Half a dozen moderate-sized lumps of sugar to every two quarts of cream tend to keep it sweet. In summer always churn twice a week. Some persons imagine that cream cannot be "too sweet," but that is a mistake; it must have a certain degree of acidity, or it will not produce butter, and if put into the churn without it, must be beaten with the paddles till it acquires it. The cream should, in the summer, be shifted each morning into a clean crock, that has first been well scalded and then soaked

---

* In very cold weather the milk-pans must be placed by the fire some time before the milk is strained into them, or the cream will not rise.

in cold water; and the same rule applies to all the utensils used in a dairy. The best things to scrub the churn and all wooden articles with, are wood ashes and plenty of soap.

In some parts of the country, the butter made by the farmers' wives for sale is not washed at all; they say, "It washes all the taste away." They remove it from the churn, and then taking it in their hands, dash it repeatedly on the board; that is what they call "smiting" it. The butter so made is always strong, and of two colors, as a portion of the buttermilk remains in it: if any of it were put into a cup, and that placed in hot water, for the purpose of clarifying, there would, when it was melted, be found a large deposit of buttermilk at the bottom of the cup. We have tried the butter made our way, and there was scarcely any residuum.

Besides, this "smiting" is a most disgusting process to witness. In warm weather the butter adheres to the hands of the "smiter," who puffs and blows over it as if it were very hard work. Indeed, I once heard a strong-looking girl, daughter of a small farmer in Kent, say she was never well, for "smiting" the butter was such dreadful hard work it gave her a pain in her side. After this "smiting" is over, it is put on a butter-print, and pressed with the hands till it is considered to have received the impression. It is then, through a small hole in the handle, blown off the print with the *mouth*.

I don't think I shall ever again eat butter which appears at table with the figures of cows, flowers, &c., stamped on it. I should always think of the process it has gone through for the sake of looking pretty. Nearly all the fresh butter which is sold in London is made up in large rolls, and, like that we make ourselves, need not be touched by the fingers of the maker.

CHAPTER V.

WHAT WE MADE BY OUR COWS.

EVERY week we kept an account of the milk and butter we consumed, and entered it in our house-keeping-book at the price we should have paid for it, supposing we had purchased the articles. We did not put down London prices, but country ones: thus, we charged ourselves with milk at 6 cents the quart, and butter 27 cents the pound; at the end of six months we made up our accounts, and found we should have paid for milk from the 14th of July to the 24th of January, $44, and $66 for butter. The food for the cows during this period cost us but $4 50, which we paid for oil-cake, of which, when the weather became cold, they had two pounds each daily. We do not reckon the value of the hay they consumed during the winter, because we included the land in our rent. We mowed three acres, which produced rather more than six loads of hay.* Getting in the crop and thatching it cost, as nearly as possible, $15, and this quantity was quite sufficient to supply the two cows—with the calf of the Strawberry, which we reared—and the pony.

An acre of grass is usually considered sufficient to support a cow during the year. If that had to be rented apart from the house, the average price would be about $25. Supposing we place that value on our land, the accounts for six months would stand thus:

EXPENSES.

Land at $25 the acre, for half a year, . .	$25 00
Oil-cake, ...	4 50
Half the expense of getting in the hay, .	7 50
	$37 00

PRODUCE.

Value of milk and butter, ...	$116 50

Leaving a balance in our favor, at the end of six months, of $79 50.

At the commencement of the winter, a cow-keeper in the neighborhood told our man that we should give

---

* We always had good crops, as the land had been always well kept. It was not " upland " hay, but our man said it had good " heart " in it for the cows.

our cows a little mangel-wurzel. We inquired, Why? and were told that we should "keep our cows better together;" so we paid a guinea for a ton of that vegetable. The first time we made butter after they had been fed with it, we found it had a very strong, bitter taste. Still, we did not condémn the mangel-wurzel, but tried it another week. The butter was again bad, so we abandoned the roots, and resolved to give the animals nothing but hay.

When they were quite deprived of green food the milk began to decrease; and as we had heard that oil-cake was given to cattle, we thought we would try some. We did so, and with complete success; we had plenty of milk, and the butter was as good as in the middle of summer, and nearly as fine a color. We did not make so much as when the cows had plenty of grass,—besides, it was now several months since the black cow had calved,—but we had sufficient for the consumption of the family. The children, it is true, did not have so many tarts as when the fruit and butter were more plentiful.

We hope that we have made all our statements clearly, and that the reader will have no difficulty in following us through this narrative of "butter-making."

Of one thing we are quite sure, that it is false economy to feed cows during the winter on anything but what we have mentioned. Grains from the brewer and distiller are extensively used by cow-keepers in large towns, but they cannot be procured in the country; and we have been told that cows fed with grains, though they may yield plenty of milk, will not make much butter.

One winter, when hay was scarce, we found that they did very well with carrots occasionally, and that they did not impart any unpleasant taste to the butter. They are likewise fond of potatoes unboiled; but these things are only required when you keep more stock than your land can support,—a fault very common to inexperienced farmers on a small scale.

CHAPTER VI.

OUR PIGS.

WE had every reason to be satisfied with the profit we had derived from our dairy, and next proceeded to examine the accounts we had kept, of our pigs for six months.

We commenced by purchasing, on the 14th of July, one for which we paid $7 50. For the first month it had nothing but the wash from the house, the skim-milk from the dairy, and greens from the garden. When we began to dig the potatoes, we found we could not hope to save the whole crop from the disease; we had, therefore, a quantity boiled and put in the pig-tub, and upon these it was fed another month. At the end of that time we began to give it a little meal and a few peas. It was killed three months after we had purchased it, and the cost for meal and peas was just $2 50. Thus, altogether, we paid for it $10, and when killed it weighed thirteen stone (182 pounds). This we reckoned worth $1 37½ the stone, which made the value of the meat $17 87½; we had, therefore, a clear profit of $7 87½. Of course, it would have been very different had we bought all the food for it; but the skim-milk, and vegetables from the garden would have been wasted, had we been without a pig to consume them: as it was, the profit arose from our " farm of four acres."

These particulars are given for the reason that the writer has frequently heard her friends in the country say, " Oh, I never keep either pigs or poultry: the pork and the fowls always cost twice the price they can be purchased for." This we could never understand, when the despisers of home-cured hams and home-fed poultry used to assert it. Supposing there was no actual profit, still it seemed strange that those who had the option of eating pork fed on milk and vegetables, and fowls which were running about the meadows a few hours before they were killed, should prefer those which are kept in close confinement and crammed with candle-graves and other abominations, till they are considered what dealers call " ripe " enough to kill; and as for pork, much of that which is sold in towns is fed on the offal from the butchers' shops, and other filth. It is well known that pigs will eat anything in the shape of animal food ; and for myself, I would much rather, like the Jew and the Turk, abjure it altogether, than partake of meat fed as pork too commonly is. How few people can eat this meat with impunity! but they might do so if the animal had been properly fed.

It is a great mistake to make pork so fat as it usually is : it is not only great waste, but deters many persons from partaking of it. Servants will not eat it, and those who purchase it, as well as those who kill their own pigs, may be certain that the surplus fat finds its way into the " wash-tub," for the benefit of a future generation of " piggies."

Our next venture proved equally fortunate. We bought three small pigs, for which we gave $3 each ; and as we wished to have pickled pork and small hams, they were killed off as we required them. The first cost $2 for barley-meal and peas, and weighed six stone, which, at $1 37½ a stone, was worth $8 25. As the cost of the pig and the food came to just $5, we had but a profit of $3 25 ; but we considered we had no right to complain: the meat was delicious, and partaken of by the children as freely as if it had been mutton.

We kept the other pigs somewhat longer, and they cost us no more for food; for, as I have already stated, they were entirely kept with the produce of our "four-acre farm," till about three weeks before they were killed. About a bushel and a half of barley meal and a peck of peas was all that was purchased for them.

The best way to ensure the healthy condition of the animals is to let them have the range of a small meadow; they should likewise be occasionally well scrubbed with soap and water. If they are thus treated, how much more wholesome must the meat be than when the poor creatures are shut up in dirty styes, and suffered to eat any garbage which is thrown to them! We always had all their food boiled. At first there was a great deal of opposition to the "muck" being introduced into the scullery; but in a little time that was overcome, and a "batch" of potatoes used to be boiled in the copper about once a month. When the skim-milk was removed from the dairy, it was taken to the "trough," and some of it mixed with a portion of the boiled potatoes, and with this food they were fed three times daily.

We have been told by a practical farmer on a larger scale, that when potatoes are not to be procured, a pig of thirty-five stone may be fattened in ten days on something less than two hundred weight of carrots. We intend to try if this is the case, and have half an acre of our orchard (which is arable) sown with carrot-seed, and feed our "stock" in the winter with the produce. With the surplus milk of two cows we find we can always keep three pigs with very little expense. Of course, if we did not plant plenty of potatoes, we must purchase more meal for them; but as we have an acre of kitchen-garden, we can very well spare half of it to grow roots for the cows and pigs. We do not reckon labor in our expenses, as we must have had a gardener, even if we had not so much spare ground, for our flower-garden and greenhouse require daily work.

We hope we have convinced those who may think of having a "little place" a few miles from town, that it may be made a source of profit as well as of amusement, and that any trouble which may be experienced by the lady superintending her own dairy and farm will be repaid by having her table well supplied with good butter, plenty of fresh eggs, (of the poultry-yard we shall speak presently,) well-cured hams, bacon, delicate and fresh pork, well-fed ducks, and chickens. All those country dainties are easily to be procured on a " farm of four acres."

Nor must another item be omitted—health ; for if you wish to be fortunate in your farming, you must look after things yourself, and that will necessitate constant exercise in the open air. We think that we have given full particulars for the management of the cow and pig.

In the next chapter we will relate our experience of the poultry-yard.

CHAPTER VII.

OUR POULTRY.

WE commenced stocking our poultry-yard in July, by purchasing twenty-eight chickens and twenty ducks, for which we paid $16 58 in the market. Some of them were too young for the table at the time we purchased them, but were all consumed at the end of four months, with the exception of seven hens and a cock, which we saved for "stock." Thus in the time I have mentioned we killed ten couple of ducks, and the same of fowls. These we entered in our housekeeping expenses at $1 37 a couple, though they were larger and better than could have been purchased in a London shop for $1 75.

We must now proceed to reckon what they cost for food, and then see if any balance remained in our favor. They consumed during the time they were getting in order for the table, three bushels of barley, at $1 25 the bushel, one bushel of meal at the same price, and one hundred weight of what is called "chicken rice," at $3 00.

The cost of the barley and meal was,	$5 00
Rice,	3 00
Cost of poultry,	16 58
Making the total price,	$24 58
Ten couple of ducks, and the same number of chickens, would amount to,	$27 50

Thus, at the first sight, it would appear that we gained but $2 92 by four months' trouble in attending to our fowl-yard; but we have now to take from the purchase money the value of the eight we saved for stock, and likewise to deduct from the barley and rice the quantity consumed by them in the four months. Now these eight were large fowls when bought, and well worth 50 cents each. We must allow for their food at least a fourth part of that consumed. We have then to take off $4 00 from the first cost of the poultry, and $2 00 from the value of the food, which will add $6 00 to the $2 92, leaving on the whole transaction a profit of $8 92.

We have still another small item to add. One of the hens we saved began to lay in the middle of

September, and by the time the four months were expired had given us two dozen eggs, which at that time of year, even in the country, were not to be procured under $37\frac{1}{2}$ cents the dozen; so that we have to add 75 cents to $8 92, making a clear profit in four months of $9 67.

It was a source of great amusement to ourselves, as well as to the children, by whom it was always considered a treat to run in the meadows, with barley in their little baskets, to the "coobiddies." When we first had the poultry we kept them in the stable-yard; but we soon found they did not thrive: they had been taken from a farm where they had the free range of the fields, and drooped in confinement, and from want of the grass and worms which they had been accustomed to feed on. We had a house constructed for them in the meadow nearest the house, and soon found that they throve much better, and did not require so much food. We had no trouble with them, except in seeing that the house was cleaned out daily. Through the fields flowed a stream of clean water, consequently our ducks throve well. The bushel of meal which figures in our accounts was for them; they used to have a little mixed in hot water once a day. We soon left it off, for we found the rice boiled in skim-milk was equally good for them, and much cheaper.

Poultry of all kinds are very fond of "scraps;" the children were always told to cut up pieces of potatoes, greens, or meat, which they might leave on their plates at the nursery dinner; and when they were removed to the kitchen, they were collected together and put into the rice-bowl for the chickens. We always fed them three times daily: in the morning with rice, in the middle of the day with "scraps," and in the evening they had just as much barley thrown to them as they cared to pick up eagerly.

We have heard some persons complain of the great expense attending a poultry-yard, but this arises from the person who has the charge of them throwing down just as much again grain as the fowls can consume. We have ourselves often seen barley trodden into the ground, if occasionally we left the task of feeding to the lad.

It must, of course, be impossible at all times for a lady to go into the fields for the purpose of feeding her chickens; the only plan to prevent waste is to have a meal-room in the house, and as much given out daily as is considered necessary for the consumption of the poultry. This is some little trouble, but will be well repaid by having at all times cheap and wholesome fowls, etc.

We have hitherto only spoken of the profit which may be obtained from a fowl-yard, when the stock is purchased. The farmer's wife, from whom we bought ours, of course gained some money by their sale. When we reared our own chickens from our own eggs, we received much more emolument from our yard; but in this little volume it is my purpose to show how a person should *commence*, who leaves London or any other large town for a suburban residence.

It must always be borne in mind, that nothing will prosper if left wholly to servants; the country proverb of "the master's eye fattens the steed," is a very true one, and another is quite as good: "the best manure you can put on the ground is the foot of the master." As a proof of our assertion we will, in the next chapter, detail the disasters we experienced when we left the charge of rabbits to the superintendence of a servant.

CHAPTER VIII.

OUR LOSSES.

OUR young people were very anxious to add some rabbits to their playthings, and as we always like to encourage a love of animals in children, we consented that they should become the fortunate shareholders in a doe and six young ones. These were bought early in September, and, as long as the weather would allow, the children used to take them food; by and by, however, one died, and then came the complaint that Master Harry had killed it by giving it too much green meat. The young gentleman was thereupon commanded not to meddle with them for the future, but the rabbits did not derive any benefit from his obedience; two or three times weekly we heard of deaths taking place in the hutch, till at last the whole half-dozen, with their mamma, reposed under the large walnut-tree.

One day the lad who had attended to them knocked

at the drawing-room door, and on entering with a large basket, drew from it a most beautiful black-and-white doe, and held it up before our admiring eyes; this was followed by the display of seven young ones, as pretty as the mother.

"Please, ma'am," said Tom, "these are the kind of rabbits you ought to have bought. My brother keeps rabbits, and these are some of his; I'll warrant they won't die!"

Willing once more to gratify the children, as well as to solve the enigma of whether it must be inevitable to lose by keeping these animals, we became the possessors of these superior creatures, with the understanding that no one was to have anything to do with them but Tom, the said Tom saying, with perfect confidence, that "he would 'warrant' they should weigh five pounds each in six weeks."

Not being learned in rabbits, we trusted to his experience and promises that we should always from that time have a brace for the table whenever we wished for them. What was our disappointment, then, when a week after we heard of the death of one of them! This was soon followed by another, and another, till the whole seven little "bunnies" shared the grave under the walnut-tree, and in a day or two the doe likewise departed: I concluded she died of grief for the loss of her offspring.

In vain did we endeavor to discover the reason of this mortality; it could not have been for want of food, for they consumed nearly as many oats as the pony. At last Tom thought of the hutch, or "locker," as he called it. "It must," said he, gravely, "have had *the* disease."

"What disease?" asked we; but we could get no other name for it than *the* disease. So what that fatal complaint among rabbits is, remains a profound mystery to us.

Now this hutch was made of new wood, in a carpenter's shop, at a cost of nearly $10, and how it could have become infected with this fearful complaint we could not comprehend. However, from that time we abandoned rabbit-keeping, and resolved not, for the future, to keep any live stock which we could not look after ourselves. We did not attempt to do so in this case, because we were frightened at the responsibility Tom threw on our shoulders, if we looked at them:

the doe always eating her young ones was one of the evils to be dreaded by our interference.

I suppose profit is to be made by keeping them, or tame rabbits would not be placed in the poulterers' hops by the side of ducks and chickens; but we are quite at a loss to know how it is accomplished. It did not much matter in a pecuniary point of view, as it was very doubtful if the children's pets would ever have died for the benefit of the dinner-table, and I only insert this chapter for the purpose of proving what I stated, viz. : that if a lady wishes her stock of any kind to prosper, she must look after it herself. When I say prosper, I mean without the expense being double the value of the produce she would receive from her " four-acre farm."

We did not enter these disasters in our kousekeeping book, it went under the title of children's expenses. For my own part, I am disposed to think that it must always be expensive to keep live stock of any kind for which all the food has to be purchased. Had we continued to keep our fowls in the yard, I am convinced they would have brought us little or no profit; but the grass, worms, and other things they found for themselves in the field, half supplied them in food, as well as keeping them healthy. We had not one death among our poultry from disease in the six months of which I have been relating this experience of our farming.

Our next venture proved more prosperous than the rabbits, and will be related in the following chapter.

CHAPTER IX.

OUR PIGEONS.

AFTER we had been a few months in the country, a friend, who was a great pigeon-fancier, wished to add some new varieties to his cote, and offered to send us, as a present, seven or eight pairs of those he wished to part with. We were greatly pleased with his offer, and at once set the carpenter at work to prepare a house for them. As soon as it was ready we received sixteen beautiful pigeons.

For the first fortnight the pigeon-holes were covered with net, that the birds might be enabled to survey at a distance their new abode, and become accustomed to the sight of the persons about the yard. When the net was removed, they eagerly availed themselves of their freedom to take flights round and round the house. One couple, of less contented disposition than the others, never came back, nor did we ever hear that they had returned to their old home. Our number was not, however, lessened by their desertion, for we received, at nearly the same time, from another friend, a pair of beautiful "pouters."

As we resolved to keep a debtor-and-creditor account of all the things we kept, we found that our eighteen pigeons consumed in every seven weeks.

Two pecks of peas	.	.	$0 75
One peck of tares	.	.	37
Ditto maize	.	.	33
			$1 45

In the first fourteen weeks we kept them, we received but two pairs of young ones, which were most mercilessly slaughtered for a pie. The price of these in the market would have been 37 cents per pair, so that we were losers on our stock; but we must say that we did not receive them till nearly the end of September, and we were agreeably surprised at finding we had young ones fit for the table at Christmas.

From that time we have been well recompensed for our peas, tares, and maize, as each couple produces on an average a pair every six weeks; thus the produce was worth $3 00, while the cost was something less than $1 50. Even had there been no profit derived, we should still have kept them, as we consider no place in the country complete without these beautiful and graceful little creatures. It was a subject of never-failing delight to the children, watching them as they wheeled round and round the house of an evening, and it was always considered a great privilege to be allowed to feed them.

At first the food was kept in the stable, and Tom was the feeder; but we were soon obliged to alter this, as we never went into the yard without treading on the corn. It was afterwards removed to the back kitchen, round the door of which they used to assemble in a flock, till one of the servants threw them out their allowance. They were considered "pets," by all the household, and were so tame that they would allow themselves to be taken in the hand and stroked.

As for the young ones, who were doomed to the *steak*, we never saw them till they made their appearance in the pie. They were taken from the nest as soon as they were fledged.

I mention this, because we were sometimes accused by our visitors (for whose especial benefit the young ones were sometimes slain) of cruelty, in eating the "pretty creatures;" but we never found that they had any scruples in partaking of them at dinner. It was usually as they were watching of a summer evening the flight of the parent birds that we were taxed with our barbarity.

We were one day much amused by a clergyman of our acquaintance, who kept a great number of these birds in a room, and who, in default of children to pet, made pets of his pigeons. At dinner, a pigeon-pie made part of the repast. This was placed opposite a visitor, who was requested to carve the dainty. He did so, and sent a portion of it to his host. The reverend gentleman looked at the plateful sent him attentively, and then said with a sigh, "I will trouble you to exchange this for part of the other bird. *This* was a peculiar favorite, and I always fed it myself. I put a mark on the breast after it was picked, for I could not bear to eat the little darling!"

We always thought that this sentimental divine had better either not have had the "little darling" put into the pie, or have swallowed his feelings and his favorite at the same time.

This dish seems to occasion wit as well as sentiment, for we were once asked by a facetious friend, " Why is a pigeon in a pie like Shakspeare's Richard III ?" We "gave it up," and were told, "Because it was bound unto the steak (stake), and could not fly." This may perhaps be a worn-out jest, but it was fresh to the writer, and so perhaps it may be to some of her readers.

We will say a few words on the management of pigeons before we conclude this chapter.

It is necessary that a pan of water should be placed in their house each day for them to wash in, and that a large lump of bay-salt should likewise be kept there. It should be occasionally cleaned out, and this is all the trouble attending keeping them. Feed them three times a day; and never throw more down than they pick up at a meal.

As I have said nothing of the profit derived from chickens when they are *reared* by the owner, so I now say nothing of the saving in keeping pigeons, when we came to sow a large patch of Indian corn, as well as some tares. We did so successfully in the acre of ground called the Orchard; and though we had abundance of fine fruit from it, the trees were not planted so thickly as to prevent any kind of crop from flourishing. But we repeat, this little book is a manual for the use of the beginner; and to such we hope it may prove both useful and encouraging.

CHAPTER X.

HOW WE CURED OUR HAMS.

I HAVE now recounted our experience in keeping cows, pigs, chickens, ducks, rabbits, and pigeons; and with everything but the rabbits we were amply satisfied with the return we received for our labor. We had a constant supply of milk, butter, eggs, ducks, chickens, and pork, not only fresh, but in the shape of good hams and bacon.

I do not know whether it is not presumptuous, in the face of Miss Acton, Mrs. Rundle, and so many other authorities, not forgetting the great Alexis Soyer, to give " our method of curing " the last-mentioned dainties; but we think we may as well follow up the history of our pigs, from the sty to the kitchen. I always found that the recipes usually given for salting pork contained too much saltpetre, which not only renders the meat hard, but causes it to be very indigestible. The following is the manner in which they were cured by ourselves:

For each ham of twelve pounds weight:
  Two pounds of common salt.
  Two ounces of saltpetre.
  ¼ pound of bay salt.
  ¼ pound of coarse sugar.

The hams to be well rubbed with this mixture, which must be in the finest powder. It is always the best plan to get your butcher to rub the meat, as a female hand is hardly heavy enough to do it effectually; they are then placed in a deep pan, and a wine-glass of vinegar is added. They should be turned each day; and for the first three or four should be well rubbed with the brine. After that time it will be sufficient, with a wooden or iron spoon, to well ladle it over the meat. They should remain three weeks in the pickle. When removed from it, they must be well wiped, put in brown-paper bags, and then smoked with *wood* smoke for three weeks.

We once had nearly a whole pig spoiled by its being taken to a baker's, where it was *dried*, but not smoked. When it came back it resembled very strong tallow.

In villages it is usual to send bacon and hams to be dried in the chimneys of farm-houses where wood is burnt, in the old-fashioned manner, on dogs; but if resident in or near a small town, there is always a drying-house to be met with, where we believe sawdust is used for fuel. We have had our own dried in this manner, and always found them excellent.

We use the same pickle for twenty-four pounds' weight of bacon, with the exception that we allow two pounds more of common salt, and when it is turned the second time the same quantity of salt is rubbed into it.

Some persons make a pickle of water, salt, sugar, and saltpetre, boiled together, and when cold put in the hams, etc., without any rubbing. We have never tried that way for meats that are to be dried, but can strongly recommend it for salt beef, pork, or mutton. The following is the pickle always used in our kitchen:

>Three gallons of *soft* water.
>One pound of coarse sugar.
>Two ounces of saltpetre.
>Three pounds of common salt.

Boil together, and let it be well skimmed; then, when cold, the meat to be well wiped and put into it. It will be fit to cook in ten days, but may be kept without injury for two months, when the pickle should be reboiled and well skimmed. The meat should be covered with brine and the pan have a cover.

We have put legs of mutton into this pickle, and can assure the reader it is an excellent mode of cooking this joint; and as it is one which frequently makes its appearance at table where the family is large, it is sometimes a pleasant method of varying the dish. It is the best way of any we know of, for curing tongues; it has the great advantage of being always ready for use, and you are not fearful of the carelessness of servants, who not unfrequently forget to look to the salting-pans.

We can recommend a dish not often seen at table, and that is a sirloin of beef put into this pickle for about a fortnight. It is infinitely superior either to the round or edgebone, and certainly not so extravagant as the last-named joint.

A friend has told us that we should procure some juniper-berries to put into our ham-pickle, but there were none to be purchased in our neighborhood, and as we were quite ignorant of the flavor they might impart, we did not trouble ourselves to get them. I am fond of old proverbs, and as our hams and bacon were always good, we determined to "let well alone."

CHAPTER XI.

OUR BREAD.

ANY lady who thinks of trying a country residence, should see that it possesses a small brick oven, for "home-made" bread ought always to be considered indispensable in the country. We did not discover that our new home was without one till after we entered it. We were laughed at by our landlord when we mentioned our want of this convenience.

"Why!" cried he, "there is a baker's shop not five minutes' walk from the house."

"Never mind," said I, "how near the baker's shop may be; we mean to have all our bread made at home. It will be, we are sure, better to do so, both on the score of health and economy."

"But I really," said the gentleman, "cannot afford to build you an oven; it would cost me $100 at the least."

At this, H., who had resided for a short time in a house where the bread was made at home, laughed, and said, " Really, Mr. L., you need not fear that we wish to put you to so much expense, and it is perhaps but fair that we should meet you half-way in the matter ; so if you will find labor we will find materials : or reverse it, if you please."

Mr. L. remembered that he had in some outhouse a quantity of " fire bricks," and it was arranged that we should pay for the labor of constructing a three-peck oven. This occasioned on our part an outlay of $10, and this small sum was the source of considerable saving to us yearly.

We were more fortunate with our bread than with our butter-making, for Mary was a capital baker ; our bread was always made from the best flour. We all liked it much better than bakers' bread, and it was much more nourishing. Indeed, when I was once in Kent during " hopping," and saw that the women who resided in the neighborhood always gave up half a day's work weekly for the purpose of going home to bake, I used to wonder why they did not purchase their bread from a baker in the village. I was informed by one of them to whom I put the question, "Lord, ma'am, we could not work on bakers' bread, we should be half-starved; it's got no *heart* in it."

To a small family, perhaps, the saving might not be considered an object, but any one who has for a few months been accustomed to eat home-made bread, would be sorry to have recourse to the baker's; the loaves purchased are usually spongy the first day, and dry and harsh the second. It is not only that other ingredients than flour, yeast, and water are mixed in the dough, but it is seldom sufficiently baked; bread well made at home and baked in a brick oven for a proper time, is as good at the end of a week as it is the second day.

I have heard several persons say, "I should like home-made bread if it were baked every day, but I don't like eating stale bread four or five days out of the seven." If they stayed with us a day or two, they became convinced that bread which had been made three or four days did not deserve the epithet of "stale."

I will now proceed to show the reader how much

flour was consumed in our household, consisting of thirteen persons.

We used to bake weekly twenty-eight pounds of flour, of the best quality; this produced *forty-two* pounds of bread. I will give in the most explicit manner I can directions for making it, which I imagine any servant will be able to comprehend:

Place in a large pan twenty-eight pounds of flour; make a hole with the hand in the centre of it like a large basin, into which strain a pint of yeast from the brewer's; this must be tasted, and if too bitter a little flour sprinkled in it, and then strained directly; then pour in two quarts of water, of the temperature of 100°, that is, what is called blood-heat, and stir the flour round from the bottom of the hole you have formed with the hand, till that part of the flour is quite thick and well mixed, though all the rest must remain unwetted; then sprinkle a little flour over the moist part, and cover with a cloth: this is called "sponge," and must be left half an hour to rise.

During this time the fire must be lighted in the oven with fagots, and the heat well maintained till the bread is ready to enter it. At the end of the half-hour add four quarts of water, of the same heat as the previous two quarts, and well knead the whole mass into a smooth dough. This is hard work, and requires strength to do it properly.

It must be again covered and left for one hour. In cold weather both sponge and dough must be placed on the kitchen-hearth, or it will not rise well.

Before the last water is put in, two table-spoonfuls of salt must be sprinkled over the flour.

Sometimes the flour will absorb another pint of water.

When the dough has risen, it must be made up into loaves as quickly as possible; if much handled then, the bread will be heavy.

It will require an hour and a half to bake it, if made into four-pound loaves.

While the dough is rising the oven must be emptied of the fire, the ashes swept from it, and then well wiped with a damp mop kept for the purpose. To ascertain if it is sufficiently heated, throw a little flour into it, and if it brown *directly*, it will do.

I think I have stated every particular necessary to enable a novice to make a " batch " of good bread.

I will sum up the articles requisite to produce forty-two pounds of the best quality :

> Flour, 28 pounds.
> Water at 100°, 12 or 13 pints.
> Two table-spoonfuls of salt.
> Yeast, 1 pint.
> Bake one hour and a half.

The quantity made was ten and a half quarterns, or four-pound loaves; and, as I have said, supplied our family of thirteen persons for the week. For the same number, when we were residing in town, the baker used to leave *thirteen* quarterns weekly.

One day, in the country, when, from the accidental absence of the bread-maker, we had to be supplied from the baker, we were surprised to hear that at the nursery-breakfast the children (six) and nurse consumed more than a two-pound loaf, and then were complaining of being " so hungry " two hours after. I thought of the words of the Kentish hopper, " that there was no heart in bakers' bread."

The servant who has the management of the oven should be instructed to take care that the wood-ashes are not thrown into the dust-hole with the ashes from the grates. They are always valuable in the country; and, as I have mentioned, the wooden articles used in the dairy should always be scrubbed with them. Should the water which is used in the house be hard, and any washing done at home, they should be placed in a coarse cloth over a tub, and water poured over them several times to make lye, which softens the water, and saves soap much more than soda, and is likewise better for the linen.

The brick oven will often prove a source of great convenience, independent of bread-making. It is just the size to bake hams or roasting pigs, and will, when dinner-parties are given, frequently prove much more useful to the cook than an extra fire.

The fagots are sold by the hundred, and the price is usually $6 25 for that quantity.

CHAPTER XII.

OUR KITCHEN-GARDEN.

AS I wish to make this little work a complete manual to the "farm of four acres," I must insert a few remarks on the management of the kitchen-garden. Ours consisted of an acre; and, large as our family was, we did not require more than half of it to supply us with vegetables, independent of potatoes.

We strongly advise any one who may have more garden than they may want for vegetables, to plant the surplus with potatoes. Even if the "disease" does affect part of the crop, the gain will still be great, providing you keep animals to consume them; for they must indeed be bad if the pigs will not thrive on them when boiled. Poultry, likewise, will eat them in preference to any other food.

We had something more than half an acre planted one year when the disease was very prevalent; the crop suffered from it to a considerable extent, but the yield was so large that we stored sufficient to supply the family from September till the end of April, and had enough of those but slightly affected to fatten four pigs, beside having a large bowlful boiled daily for the poultry. The worst parts were always cut out before they were boiled, and neither pigs nor poultry were allowed to touch them raw.

It is much the best plan to consume all the potatoes you may grow, rather than save any of them for seed. It will be but a slight additional expense to have fresh kinds sent from quite a different locality, and they will thrive better, and not be so liable to the disease.

They should always be dug before the slightest appearance of frost, and placed on straw in a dry place, where they can be conveniently looked over once a fortnight, when any that show symptoms of decay should be removed and boiled at once for the pigs. By this method very few will be wholly wasted; instead of eating potatoes you will eat pork, that is, if you have plenty of skim-milk. I do not at all know how pigs would like them without they were mixed up with that fluid.

We have tried, with great success, planting them in rows alternately with other vegetables. When they are all together, the haulms in wet seasons grow so rankly that they become matted together; and then, as the air is excluded from the roots, it renders them liable to disease. We have tried cutting the haulm off to within a few inches of the ground; but this, the gardener said, proved detrimental to the roots. We afterwards tried a row of potatoes, then cabbages, then carrots, and then again came the potatoes. We once planted them between the currant and gooseberry bushes, but it was as bad, or worse, than when a quantity of them were by themselves; for when the trees made their midsummer shoots the leaves quite shut out air and light from the potatoes, and when dug they proved worse than any other portion of the crop.

We always found that the deeper the sets were placed in the ground the sounder were the roots. We tried every experiment with them; and as our gardener was both skilful and industrious, we were usually much more fortunate with our produce than our neighbors.

Carrots rank to the "small farmer" next in value to the potatoes: not only pigs and cows are fond of them, but likewise horses. The pony always improved in condition when he was allowed to have a few daily.

Our arable acre was a model farm on a very small scale. We grew in it maize for the poultry, tares for the pigeons, lucerne for the cows, and talked of oats for the pony. This our gardener objected to, so the surplus bit of ground was sown with parsnips, which turned out very profitable, as both pigs and cows liked them.

We have told the reader that we reared the calf of the Strawberry cow, and it cost us hardly anything to do so, for it was fed in the winter with the roots we had to spare. The first winter it had to consume the greater part of the ton of mangel-wurzel we had bought "to keep our cows together." Some we had boiled with potatoes for the pigs, and they liked it very well.

An acre of land may appear a laughably small piéce of ground to produce such a variety of articles, but if well attended to, the yield will astonish those who are ignorant of gardening. The one important thing to be attended to is, to see that all seed-crops are well thinned out as soon as they are an inch above the surface. In very few kitchen-gardens is this attended to, and for want of this care a dozen carrots, parsnips, or turnips, are allowed to stand where one would be sufficient. The one would prove a fine root; the dozen are not worth the trouble of pulling, as they can get neither air nor room to grow. To be well done they should be thinned by hand, and that being a tedious "job," gardeners seldom can be induced to perform the work properly.

As our ground became productive we added another cow, and more pigs and poultry, but I shall not now say with what success. This little book is only intended for the novice in farming, and details only the results of the first six months of our "farm of four acres."

Perhaps I should have called it *five* acres, as nearly the whole of the acre of kitchen-garden was devoted to the cultivation of food for our "stock."

We had a very broad sunny border at the back of the flower-garden, which grew nearly all the spring and summer vegetables we required : such as seakale, early potatoes, peas, cauliflowers, and salads.

We have not yet said anything of the money we saved by our kitchen-garden, but we must add to the profits of our six months' farming the average amount we should have paid to a green-grocer for fruit and vegetables.

Twenty-five cents a day to supply thirteen persons with these necessary articles is certainly not more than must have been expended. Still, $90 per annum is a considerable item of household expenditure, and scanty would have been the supply it would have furnished; as it was we had a profusion of fruit of all kinds, from the humble gooseberry and currant to the finest peaches, nectarines, and hothouse grapes, as well as an abundant supply of walnuts and filberts.

Had we bought all the produce of our garden, the value would have more than paid our gardener's wages.

Nor must I omit the luxury of having beautiful flowers from the greenhouse throughout the winter; these superfluous items did not figure in our accounts. We should have purchased nothing but bare necessaries, and therefore entered but twenty-five cents a day for "garden stuff" in our housekeeping book.

Those only who have lived in the country can appreciate the luxury of not only having fruit and vegetables in abundance, but of having them fresh. Early potatoes fresh dug, peas fresh gathered, salad fresh cut, and fruit plucked just before it makes its appearance at table, are things which cannot be purchased by the wealthiest residents in a great city.

Not far from our residence there were large grounds, which were cultivated with fruit and vegetables for the London market. I have frequently seen the wagons packed for Covent Garden. The freshest that can be procured there would be considered "stale" in the neighborhood in which they were grown. Any fruit or vegetables in that far-famed market must have been gathered twenty-four hours before they could find their way into the kitchen of the consumer; and it is not only the time which has elapsed, but the manner in which they are packed, which so much deteriorates their quality.

Have any of our readers ever seen the densely-loaded wagons which enter that market? The vegetables are wedged as closely together as they can be pressed, which very soon causes, in warm weather, cabbages, greens, &c., to ferment and become unwholesome. I have often seen them so loaded in the middle of the day before they reached London. They are left in the hot sun till the time arrives, when the horses are placed in them, and they begin their slow journey towards town. This is seldom till late at night when the distance does not exceed a dozen miles.

The finer kinds of fruit, such as peaches, grapes, etc., do not injure so much by being kept a few days before they are eaten; indeed, *ripe* peaches and nectarines are seldom gathered for sale: they would spoil too quickly to enable the fruiterer to realize much profit. They are plucked when quite hard, and then placed in boxes till they gradually *soften;* but the flavor of fruit thus treated is very inferior to that of a peach or nectarine ripened by the sun. Seed-fruits, such as strawberries, become very vapid in four or five hours after they have been picked, if they were then quite ripe.

I know that the last few pages have nothing to do with "the money we made" by our farm, but I wish to show the reader all the advantages which a country residence possesses over a town one. Some persons, who cannot live without excitement, think that nothing can compensate for the want of amusement and society.

I was once speaking of the pleasure I experienced from residing in the country, and placed *health* among its many advantages, when I was answered, "It is better to die in London than live in the country!"

I think I have said enough to cause my lady readers to wish that the time may not be far distant when they may, like ourselves,—for we did all sorts of "odd jobs" in our garden,—cut their own asparagus, and assist in gathering their own peas.

It is indeed impossible to over-estimate the value of a kitchen-garden in a large family which numbers many children among its members.

CHAPTER XIII.

THE MONEY WE MADE.

SOME time ago we showed our first six months' accounts to a friend, who was very sceptical as to the profit we always told him we made by our farming. After he had looked over our figures, he said,—

"Well! and after all, what have you made by your butter-making, pig-killing, and fowl-slaughtering?"

"What have we made?" said I, indignantly. "Why, don't you see that, from July to January, we realized a profit of $9 50 from our cows, $11 12 from our pigs, $9 67 from our poultry-yard, and $45 at the least from our kitchen-garden, which, altogether, amounts to no less a sum than $145 29; and all this in our 'salad-days, when we were green in judgment?' What shall we not make now that we have more stock, our ground well cropped, and, better still, have gained so much experience?"

"Well," said our friend, "the more 'stock,' as you call it, you have, the more money you will lose."

At this rejoinder, H. looked at the speaker as if she thought he had "eaten of the insane root, which takes the reason prisoner."

"*Lose more money!* when you can yourself see, by looking at this book, that in our first six months we have cleared $145 29! And, indeed, it was absurd of A. to put down so little, for she has allowed $25 for the land; and if she take that off the rent, she ought to enter it as profit from the "farm." Besides, think of only putting down a shilling a day for fruit and vegetables! Very few puddings would the children get at that rate, supposing we were in London."

"If we were in London," interrupted I, "you know that $90 yearly would be as much as we could afford to expend for that item in our family. I have made out all our farming accounts as fairly as I can. I am a swell aware as you can be that a shilling a day would not give us the luxuries of the garden as we now have them; and though that plenty may form one of the advantages of residing in the country, we have no right to put down as a saving of money the value of articles we should never have thought of purchasing."

"I must allow," said Mr. N., "that you appear to have been strictly honest in your entries as regards the value of the produce you have received, but you do not appear to have put down your losses. You keep a one-sided ledger. You have the credit, but not the debit entry. You say nothing of the money you have lost by pigeons and rabbit-keeping."

Now the utmost we had lost by our pigeons in the six months was $2 25, and he knew perfectly well how profitable they had since been to us. He used jokingly to say, that we fed our guests with them in every mode of cookery so frequently, that they would alter the old grace of "for rabbits hot," &c., and substitute the word "pigeon" in its place; so we thought it was ungenerous to reproach the poor birds with the scanty number they gave us the first few weeks they were in our dove-cote.

Silenced on that point, he returned to our unfortunate rabbit speculation, and complained that we had kept no account of the money we had lost by them.

Here H. stopped him by saying,

"Pray, Mr. N., did you not purchase your children a pony, and did it not catch cold and die in a month afterwards? I suppose Mrs. N. did not enter that in her housekeeper's book as meat at so much a pound, and why should we put down the cost of the rabbits in our farming accounts? No; of course it was entered among the 'sundries.'"

"But you must allow," said Mr. N., "that if you had done as I advised you, and taken a house in a street leading into one of the squares, you would have lived more cheaply than here. Why, your gardener's wages must more than swallow up any profit which you may *think* you make from your farm. You must acknowledge you would have saved that expense."

"Granted," said I; "but we should most likely have paid quite as much to a doctor. We never got through a year in town without a heavy bill to one; and we must have had all the expense and trouble of taking the children out of town during the hot weather, while they have had excellent health ever since they have been here; and with the exception, when some kind friend like yourself has asked one of them on a visit, neither of them has left home since we came here. Of one thing I am quite sure, that we are much happier than we should have been in London; and that in every point of view, as regards expenditure, we are gainers. I have not entered any profit arising from baking at home, though the difference is just three four-pound loaves weekly; and Mrs. N. will tell you what must be the saving by our having our own laundry."

"Enough! enough!" said Mr. N., laughingly; "your evidence is overwhelming. You almost force me to believe that I could live in the country, feed my own pork, and drink my own milk, without paying half a crown a pound for the one or a shilling a quart for the other, and this was what I never before believed possible; and I am quite sure, that if I were to put the assertion in a book, no one would believe me."

"Then," exclaimed I, "it shall be asserted in a book whenever I can find time to transcribe all the particulars from my diary; and I hope that I may be able to convince my readers—should I be fortunate enough to obtain any—not only that they may keep cows, pigs, and poultry without loss, but that they may derive health, recreation, and profit from doing so. None know better than yourself how worn-out in health and spirits we were when we came to this place; how oppressed with cares and anxieties. Without occupation, we should most likely have become habitual invalids, real or fancied; without some inducement to be out of doors, we should seldom have exerted ourselves to take the exercise necessary to restore us to health and strength. But you will lose your train, if I keep you longer listening to the benefits we have experienced by our residence in this place. Give the fruit and flowers to Mrs. N. with our love; and tell her, that with God's blessing we have improved in 'mind, body, and estate,' by occupying ourselves with ' our farm of four acres.'"

CHAPTER XIV.

THE NEXT SIX MONTHS.

IT was not my intention when I commenced this little work to do more than give our first six months' experience in farming our four acres of land; but as perhaps the reader may think that time hardly sufficient to form a correct opinion of the advantages to be derived from a residence in the country, I think it as well to add some particulars relating to the following six months.

In the spring came a new source of profit and amusement. We commenced our labors in the poultry-yard in February, by setting a hen on thirteen eggs, which, early in March, produced the same number of chickens: these were all ready for the table in the middle of May. At that time we could not have purchased them under $1 50 the couple.

The cost of thirty-eight chickens till ready to kill was $4 37. We always knew exactly the expense attending the poultry, because we had a separate book from the miller, in which every article was entered as it came into the house ; and as the chickens were kept distinct from the other fowls, I could tell the exact sum they had cost us when they made their appearance at table.

The first thing that was given them to eat was egg, boiled quite hard, chopped very fine, and mixed with bread-crumbs. After that they had groats. I find they consumed :

Three quarts of whole groats	$ 37
Two bushels of barley	2 25
One bushel of middlings	1 12
Twenty-five lbs. of chicken-rice	63
Making altogether	$4 37

The reader must be told that those thirty-eight chickens had other things to eat than those I have put down ; they had nearly all the scraps from the house, consisting of cold potatoes, bits of meat, pudding, &c., and any pieces of bread which were left at table were soaked in skim-milk ; and the rice was also boiled in it. Of course, in a smaller family there would not have been so many " scraps " for them; but, however strict you may be with children, you cannot prevent their leaving remnants on their plates, all of which would have been wasted had it not been for the chickens and pig-tub.

We were not so fortunate with the ducks. We did not keep any through the winter, consequently we had to purchase the eggs, which were placed under hens; for those eggs we paid four cents each, and out of thirteen, which was the number given to each hen, we never reared more than eight ducks.

Thus, in the first instance, they cost us six cents each; and they were likewise more expensive to feed than the chickens. They were never fit for the table till they had cost us sixty-three cents the couple. One reason of this was, that as the chickens had all the waste bits, they had nothing but what was bought for them; but then they were such ducks as could not have been purchased at the poulterers'.

We never killed one unless it weighed four pounds; they used to be brought in at night, and placed in the scale: if it was the weight I have mentioned it was killed, if not it was respited till it did so.

At first we tried cooping them to fatten, but found

it did not answer, as they moped and refused to eat by themselves; so we abandoned that plan, and were content to let them run in the meadows till fit to kill, which was not till they were three months old. They were never "fat," but very meaty, and fine flavored, —not in the least like those which are bought, which, however fat they may appear before they are cooked, come to table half the size they were when put down to the fire.

I remember being rather puzzled once when resident in London. I wanted a particularly fine couple of ducks for a "company dinner," and went myself to the shop where I dealt to order them.

"Now, Mrs. Todd," said I, "the ducks I require are not fat ducks, but meaty ones; the last I had from you had nothing on them when they came to table, though they looked so plump when you sent them."

"Oh, yes, ma'am," was the rejoinder. "I know just what you want; but they are very difficult to get: you want *running* ducks."

I was obliged to ask what she meant by the term *running*, and was then informed that the ducks for the London market were put up to fatten, and as they were crammed with grease to hasten the process, the fat all went into the dripping-pan. Now a *running* duck was one well fed, and allowed to roam or *run* till it was killed. I am now able from experience to say, that they are incomparably superior to their fattened brethren.

The novice in poultry-rearing must be told that it is almost useless to set a hen in very hot weather. As we had more eggs than were required, we did so during part of June, July, and August, but had very bad fortune with them; the hen seldom hatching more than three or four, and those puny little creatures.

There is an old Kentish proverb which says,

> "Between the sickle and the scythe,
> Whatever's born will never thrive;"

and as it was just between the hay and corn-harvest that we tried to rear our ducks and chickens, I am induced to believe that, like many other old saws, it was founded on experience. They may be reared in September, though they require great care, and must not be allowed to run on the grass, which at that season is seldom dry.

A friend once told me she reared a brood of seventeen chickens, which were hatched the last week in September; they were placed in an empty greenhouse, and were consequently kept warm and dry. March is *the* month for poultry; the hatches are better, and they grow much more rapidly than at any other time.

I am quite sure that a poultry-yard may be made very profitable to any one who will bestow a little trouble on it. Great care must be taken with the young chickens at night; the hen should be securely cooped with them: for want of this precaution we in one night lost eight, when they were a few days old, being, as we supposed, carried off by the cats.

The best food for ducks when first hatched is bread and milk; in a few days barley-meal, wetted with water into balls about as big as peas, should be given to them. It is usual, as soon as both ducks and chickens come out of the shell, to put a pepper-corn down their throats. I don't know that it is really of service to them, but it is a time-honored custom, and so perhaps it is as well to follow it.

As for our butter-making, it continued to prosper; we had some little trouble with it in the spring, when the weather set in suddenly very hot. It was certainly much more difficult to reduce the temperature of the cream to 55° than it was to raise it to that degree.

I often thought with vain longing of the shop in the Strand, where we used to purchase Wenham Lake Ice : how firm would the butter have come, could we have had a few lumps to put in the churn half an hour before we required to use it!

Farmers' wives tell us, that to get firm butter in very hot weather they get up at three o'clock in the morning, in order that it may be made before the sun becomes powerful. Now this is a thing that would not have suited H. or myself at all, and therefore we never mustered up courage to attempt it.

One day in March—and this is the last disaster I have to record concerning our butter—we were particularly anxious to have it good, as we expected visitors, to whom we had frequently boasted of our skill as dairywomen : the day was very warm, and the cream appeared much thicker than usual ; we churned for more than an hour without its appearing to undergo any change ; we frequently removed the lid to see if there was any sign of butter coming, but each time we were disheartened when we discovered it looked just the same as when placed in the churn. At last the handle went round as easily as if no cream were in it, and presently it began to run over the top of the churn. When we looked in a curious sight presented itself: the cream had risen to the top, just as milk does when it boils! We were greatly astonished. In nine months' butter-making we had seen nothing like it.

Tom, who milked the cows, was supposed to know something of the art of churning; he was, therefore, called into the dairy: as soon as he saw the state of the matter he exclaimed, " Why, the cream's gone to sleep!"

" The cream gone to sleep!" What in the world could that mean? Such a propensity we had never discovered in cream before; we could gain no solution of the mystery from Tom; all he said was, that we must go on churning till it " waked up."

H. and myself had been hard at work for two hours, so willingly yielded to his request that he might be allowed to rouse the cream from its slumber. He, the cook, and housemaid, churned away by turns till seven in the evening, but the sleep of the cream remained unbroken, and as it was then considered a hopeless affair, the slothful fluid was consigned to the pig-tub.

Now we have never felt quite sure of our butter since. Every time we churn there is a lurking fear that the cream may choose to take a nap; however, it is as yet the first and last time in our experience.

I can give no advice to my readers on the subject, because I am wholly ignorant on the subject, though I have consulted every farmer's wife in the neighborhood on the matter. They all say that cream will go to sleep sometimes, though it usually wakes up after a few hours.* Perhaps, after all, we were too impatient, and should not have given in after *only* nine hours' churning. With this solitary exception our butter-making progressed -as favorably as we could desire.

I do not quite know how to believe the stories I am told of wonderful cows which my friends are fortunate

---

* I have since been told by an old woman conversant with sleepy cream, that a quart of milk nearly boiling hot will wake it up.

enough to possess. One gentleman has informed me that he has one which gives fifteen pounds of butter weekly. Now we have had several, but never made more on the average than eight pounds per week. I believe that a great deal depends on the manner in which they are milked, and once in the hands of a beginner in that art the cows decreased in milk so rapidly, that we did not get more than a gallon daily from both animals; after they had been three weeks under his management we changed the milker, but did not get anything like the proper quantity again till after they had calved.

I believe the usual average is one pound of butter from every ten quarts of milk. Ours used to give us thirteen or fourteen quarts each daily, and yet we never made more than eight pounds. We used about two quarts of new milk, so that if ten quarts will give a pound of butter, we did not get so much as we ought. Still we were very well satisfied with the produce we received.

There requires management with two cows, in order that one may always be in full milk when the other calves. If you rear a calf for the butcher, it will require the whole of the milk for six or seven weeks, which is about the age they are killed for fine veal. We once—it was in the winter—received $26 for one. With two cows this may usually be done, and it is more profitable than making butter. Where only one is kept, it is better to part with the calf when a few days old, and then the price is $5.

If a lady wishes her dairy to be very nicely furnished, she should have all the articles she requires of glass, instead of wood and earthenware. Everything for the dairy of that material can be purchased in Leicester Square, and certainly, if expense had been no object to us, we should much have preferred a glass churn, pans, &c. They have the great advantage of being kept beautifully clean with very little labor; but they are so liable to be broken, that they should never be used unless servants are very careful. A marble table is, however, in every respect better than a board to make the butter upon. It is expensive at first, but will, with ordinary care, last several generations of butter-makers.

Whilst on the subject of the dairy, I must say a few words respecting the great care required in washing the articles used in it. As soon as the butter was taken from the churn I was in the habit of half filling it with boiling water, into which I had put some lumps of soda, and then turning the handle a few times, in order that it might be well washed round. It was then left till it was convenient for "cook" to cleanse all the utensils we had used.

From some cause or other I neglected for two or three weeks to do this, and one day, when the fresh-made butter was brought to table, there were complaints that it was *cheesy;* it certainly had a peculiar and very unpleasant taste, for which we could not account.

The next time it was made it had the same fault; and it then occurred to me that it might be the churn. I accordingly returned to my old mode of washing it, and never after was there a complaint of any unpleasant flavor in the butter.

I mention this to show the amateur dairywoman how very essential is cleanliness in every article she uses. A regular dairymaid would have known this, but a town-servant thinks that if she washes a thing it is sufficient: but more than mere washing is required; every article must be *scrubbed* with soap, wood-ashes, and soda, and then placed for hours in the open air.

Now glass is much easier kept sweet and clean, and for that reason is greatly to be preferred; but I am writing for those who may wish to reap profit from their " farm of four acres," and I fear little would be gained if nothing but glass were used in the dairy.

Our land turned out better the second summer than the first. We made nearly two tons and a half of hay from each acre. We were enabled to mow the whole three acres, as we had " common rights " in our neighborhood, where the cows could pasture during the spring. Had we been without this privilege we could have mown only two acres, and as hay was $21 the load, the additional acre was worth $50 to us, with the exception of $3 75 for making it. We were advised to have an after-crop, but did not; it would have made the land very poor for the next year, so that what we gained in hay we must have expended in manure.

We were well satisfied with the profit we derived from our pigs during this second six months. All the summer we kept four, at an expense of fifty-eight cents weekly, which was expended for two bushels of fine pollard (bran and meal).

We had such an abundance of vegetables from the garden and orchard, that we must have wasted cartloads, if we had not kept pigs to consume them. As soon as the hay was carried they were turned into the meadows, and suffered to remain there till they were put up to fatten; a process which pigs must go through, though ducks can dispense with it. I have already stated the expense of fattening them, and we never found it vary more than a shilling or two in a pig.

We always found for our family that a bacon pig of sixteen stone (224 pounds) was the best size, and for porkers about eight (112 pounds).

Our fruit was as plentiful as our vegetables,—indeed, we might have sold the surplus for many dollars; but we soon found that to do so was to lose *caste* in the neighborhood. One piece of extravagance we were guilty of the first winter and spring we passed at A. The gardener had a little fire in the grapery during the severe weather, because he had placed some plants in it. We were told we could continue it till the grapes ripened for a "mere nothing." Now "mere nothings" mount up to a "considerable something." The coal and coke consumed before they were ripe cost $20. It is true we had them in July instead of September, but we should have liked them quite as well in that month.

It was a bad grape year, too,—at least with us. I don't think we cut more than twenty pounds weight. Hothouse grapes are not dear at $1 the pound; but we should have had them equally good by waiting two months later, when they would have cost us nothing.

Had we purchased the produce we received from our garden during the year, it would have been worth two guineas weekly. Our peaches, apricots, and nectarines, were abundant, and very fine. We had two splendid walnut-trees, and a mulberry-tree of immense size, which was an object of special abhorrence to "nurse," as for more than two months in the summer the children's frocks, pinners, &c., were dyed with the juice of the fruit. They could hardly pass near it in the season without some of the ripe berries falling on their heads, and it was hardly possible to prevent them escaping from her to pick them up. Mulberry-pudding made its appearance often on the nursery-table, and jars of mulberry-jam were provided to secure the same dainty through the winter.

The luxury of a good garden can hardly be appreciated till you have been in possession of one, more especially where there are many children. The way we used to preserve currants, gooseberries, plums, damsons, and, indeed, almost every description of fruit, was this: The wide-mouth bottles which are sold for the purpose were filled with fruit, six ounces of powdered loaf-sugar was shaken in among it; the bottles were then tied down as closely as possible with bladder, and placed up to the neck in a copper, or large saucepan, of cold water, which was allowed to come slowly to the boil. They remained in it till the water was quite cold, when they were taken from the water and wiped quite dry. Before placing them in the store-room the bottle was turned upside down, in order to see that they were perfectly air-tight, for on this depends the fruit keeping good. The fruit will sink down to about the middle of the bottle, and we once tried to fill them up with some from another, but opening them admitted the air, and the contents did not keep well. If properly done, they will be good at the end of a year.

If any lady undertake the management of a four-acre farm, she must expect it to occupy a great deal of her time; if she leaves it to servants, however honest, she will lose by it. It is not that things are stolen, but that they are wasted, unless the mistress herself knows what quantities of barley, oats, etc., her poultry and pigs consume; and unless she look daily into her dairy and see that the milk is well skimmed, half the cream will be thrown into the wash-tub.

A six-months' longer experience of the country only confirmed my sister and myself in the conviction that we had in every way made a most desirable change when we quitted London for our small farm; but if we had been too fine or too indolent to look after our dairy and poultry-yard, I believe that our milk, butter, eggs, poultry, and pork, would have cost us quite as much as we could have purchased them for in town.

All the good things we were daily consuming in the country would have come to us in London,

"Like angels' visits, few and far between."

I know that many of our old friends were really shocked when we told them, laughingly, of our new pursuits, and that the butter they so much praised, and the apricot-cheese they ate with so much gusto, were manufactured by our own hands. We were "poor-thinged" to our faces in a very pitying manner, but we always laughed at these compassionate people, and endeavored to convince them we spoke the truth in sober earnest, when we assured them we found great amusement in our new pursuits. They shook their heads and sighed in such a manner, that we knew perfectly well that, as soon as we were out of ear-shot, they would say, "Poor things! it is very sad, but they are quite right to try and make the best of it." I believe some of them thought that it was impossible we could have " souls above butter ;" for a lady who called one day, taking up one of Mudie's volumes from the table, said,—

"Is it possible you care to subscribe to Mudie's?"

" And why should we not care to do so ?" replied H.

" Why," was the answer, " I do not see any connection between a love of reading and a love of butter-making."

Now I do not think that either of us had any love of butter-making ; and if we could have afforded to give $100 a year to a dairymaid, no doubt we should have left all to her management ; but as it was we were obliged to buy it—and very bad it was in our town—or make it ourselves : nor do either my sister or myself regret our resolution to do so.

At first we were quite proud of our skill, and told every one of our success with great triumph. Now—for womanhood is weak—we are content to hear our dairymaid praised for her beautiful butter by our acquaintance, and Tom extolled for his care of the chickens. It is only our friends, among whom I reckon my readers, who know that the butter is made, and the chickens fed, by the mistresses of " the four-acre farm."

CHAPTER XV.

OUR PONY.

I HAVE been told by several friends that, in order to render this little book complete, I should add a chapter detailing the expenses we incurred by keeping a pony and carriage. Some persons imagine that this is an article of luxury which may well be dispensed with; but, though it may not be an absolute necessary, the expense attending one is so slight, in comparison with the comfort and pleasure derived from its possession, that I believe such of my readers as may contemplate residing in the country will readily agree with me, when I have told them the amount it will cost them to keep it,—that if it is a luxury, it is one of the very cheapest in which they can indulge.

Without such a convenience a carriage must be hired every time any member of the family has occasion to go to the railway station; and besides that, it is useful for bringing home a variety of articles which in the country are frequently purchased at places five or six miles from home. Then it is a great pleasure to be able to meet your friends at the station, whenever they are kind enough to leave London for the purpose of passing a few days with you in the country.

My sister and myself contrived to extract profit as well as pleasure from our little equipage. During the summer months we frequently drove up to London; the short journey was very pleasant, and this mode of making it possessed the great advantange of costing nothing but 63 cents for the pony, and 12 cents for turnpikes. Not that we had the temerity to drive through London. We always left the pony two miles before we reached town, with strict orders to the civil ostler to whose care we confided him to take great care of him, and be sure and give him a " good feed." We then proceeded on our way in a cab, which cost us no more than we should have paid for one from the station.

Where there is a gentleman in the family, a dog-cart is the most convenient vehicle which can be kept; but as that would not be suitable for a lady, we contrived to make the back seat of the carriage do duty for the well of the dog-cart, and it was astonishing how many light packages we managed to " stow "away" in it. I will not dilate on the pleasant drives through quiet lanes, of the delight afforded to the children when allowed to have a ride on "Bobby," nor of the great facility it gave us of being out of doors in winter, when, as was very frequently the case, the state of the roads was such as to render walking an impossibility; still, I hope I have stated sufficient to give my readers a good idea of the great pleasure they will derive from keeping a pony; and I will now, with the bills of the miller and farrier before me, proceed to show the sum for which it may be kept. Our pony cost for food, from the 4th of January to the 24th of December in the same year, $46.66. He consumed during that period five quarters of oats, at $8 the quarter, and five bushels of beans, which cost $6.66. The farrier's bill for the same time amounted to $5.91. Perhaps it will be as well to copy this account, as it will clearly show how often it is requisite to change the shoes of a horse. Of course a great deal must depend on the quantity of work he does; ours was certainly not spared, though we do not deserve the character so usually given to ladies, of being unmerciful to horses: "running them off their legs," "thinking they can never get enough out of the poor beasts," "driving them as if they thought they could go for ever," are the accusations brought against the ladies of a family where horses are kept.

The following is a copy of the bill for our pony's shoes for twelve months :—

Feb. 24. Four removes	$0.33
March 22. Four shoes	.75
April 20. Four removes	.33
May 5. Two shoes	.37½
June 9. Four shoes	.75
July 8. Four shoes	.75
Aug. 9. Four shoes	.75
Sept. 1. Four shoes	.75
Oct. 11. Two shoes	.37½
Oct. 25. Two shoes	.27½
Dec. 24. Two shoes	.37½
	$ 5.91
Add to this the miller's bill	$46.66
	$52.57

and we have the whole expense of keeping a pony for one year. "Oh! but," some one may exclaim, "you have put down nothing for straw and hay, and horses require a great deal of both." Quite true; but then in the country, if you do not keep a horse, you must buy manure for your garden, and that will cost you quite as much as if you purchased straw; and as for the hay, did it not come off the " four-acre farm?"

It is one of the great advantages of the country that nothing is lost, and thus the straw which figures so largely in the bill of a London corn-chandler, and which, when converted into manure, is the perquisite of your groom, becomes in the country the means of rendering your garden productive.

Before I resided in the country the pony cost me more than four times the sum I have mentioned; the stable was apart from the house, and I knew nothing for months of the bills run up on his account. I had once a bill sent in for sugar! " Why, George, what can the pony want with sugar?"

" Why, ma'am, you said some time ago that the pony looked thin, so lately I have always mixed sugar with his corn; nothing fattens a horse like sugar."

Now what could I complain of? This man had been recommended to me as a "treasure," and one who would do his duty by the pony, which, I may mention, was a very beautiful one, and a great pet; so if George considered sugar good for him, what could I do but pay the bill, and say, " Let him have sugar, by all means"? Not that "Bobby" was a bit the fatter or better for having his corn sweetened. An intimate friend of mine, who always kept three or four horses, laughed outright when I told him that the pony had consumed such a quantity of sugar, and expressed his opinion that very little of that article had ever been in his manger. Under the same superintendence "Bobby" wore out four times the number of shoes; and as at that time I had to purchase hay and straw as well as corn, all on the same scale of magnitude, the expense of keeping the little carriage really did cost more than the convenience attending it was worth; and had not the pony been the gift of a beloved friend, we should have parted with it when we quitted London, as at that time we were ignorant how cheaply it could be maintained in the country. There we had a servant who was content with his wages, and did not seek to make them greater by combining with tradesmen to defraud his employers. If any of my readers commence keeping a pony in the country, they may rely that it need not cost them a penny more than I have put down. Of course they must have the hay from their own grounds, and neither reckon the cost of the straw nor the labor of the man who attends to the pony. Ours did all the "jobs" about the place—cleaned the knives and shoes, milked the cows, fed the pigs and poultry, helped in the gardens, and, in short, made himself "generally useful." Now, a servant who is able and willing to do all this, besides properly attending to a pony and carriage, is very difficult to be met with, but he is absolutely necessary for a place in the country where economy has to be studied.

Something must be allowed yearly for the wear and tear of carriage, harness, etc., but it need not be much. Any gentleman can easily calculate the sum which may fairly be allowed for these items; I only think it my part to show the expense attending a pony in the country; and though those who have been in the habit of keeping horses in London, either in a livery or private stable, may think it impossible to maintain one for $52 57 yearly, let them leave town for a four-acre farm, and they will find that I have spoken the truth on this point, as well as on all the other subjects of which I have given my experience in this little volume.

CHAPTER XVI.

CONCLUSION.

IT is with considerable diffidence the writer ventures to give the public this slight sketch of her experience in farming four acres of land.

When she finally resolved to fix her residence in the country, she was wholly ignorant how she ought to manage, so that the small quantity of land she rented might, if not a source of profit, be at least no loss.

She was told by a friend, who for a short time had tried "a little place" at Chiselhurst, that it was very possible to lose a considerable sum yearly by undertaking to farm a very small quantity of land. "Be quite sure," said the friendly adviser—"and remember, I speak from experience—that whatever animals you may keep, the expense attending them will be treble the value of the produce you receive. Your cows will die, or, for want of being properly looked after, will soon cease to give any milk; your pigs will cost you more for food than will buy the pork four times over; your chickens and ducks will stray away, or be stolen; your garden-produce will, if worth anything, find its way to Covent Garden; and each quarter your bills from the seedsman and miller will amount to as much as would supply you with meat, bread, milk, butter, eggs, and poultry, in London."

Certainly this was rather a black state of things to look forward to; but the conviction was formed, after mature reflection, that a residence some miles from town was the one best suited to the writer's family. She was compelled to acknowledge to those friends who advised her to the contrary, her ignorance on most things appertaining to the mode of life she proposed to commence, but trusted to that often-talked-of commodity, common sense, to prevent her being ruined by farming four acres of land.

She thought, if she could not herself discover how to manage, she might acquire the requisite knowledge from some of the little books she had purchased on subjects connected with "rural economy." They proved, however, quite useless. They appeared to the writer to be merely compilations from larger works; and, like the actors in the barn, who played the tragedy of "Hamlet," and omitted the character of the hero, so did these books leave out the very things which, from the title-pages, the purchaser expected to find in them.

Some time after experience had shown how butter could be made successfully, a lady, who had been for years resident in the country, said, during a morning call, "My dairy-maid is gone away ill, and the cook makes the butter; but it is so bad we cannot eat it: and besides that nuisance, she has this morning given me notice to leave. She says she did not 'engage' to 'mess' about in the dairy."

"Well," said the writer, "why not make the butter yourself, till you can suit yourself with a new servant?"

"I have tried," said the visitor, "but cannot do it. My husband is very particular about the butter being good, so I was determined to see if I could not have some that he could eat; therefore I *pored* over Mrs. Rundle, and other books, for a whole day, but could not find how to begin. None of them told me how to *make* the butter, though several gave directions for potting it down when it was made. I made the boy churn for more than three hours yesterday morning, but got no butter after all. *It would not come!*"

The weather was very cold, and it occurred to the listener to ask the lady *where* the boy churned, and where the cream had been kept during the previous night.

"Why, in the dairy, to be sure," was the answer; "and my feet became so chilled by standing there, that I can hardly put them to the ground since. Cook could not succeed more than I did, and said, the last time she made it, it was between four and five hours before the butter came; and then, as I have told you, it was not eatable."

The writer explained to her friend that the reason why she could not get the butter, as well as why cook's was so bad, was on account of the low temperature of the cream when it was put into the churn. She then gave her plain directions how to proceed for the future, and was gratified by receiving a note from her friend, in a couple of days, containing her thanks for the " very plain directions ; " and adding, " I could not have thought it was so little trouble to procure *good* butter, and shall for the future be independent of a saucy dairymaid."

I believe that a really clever servant will never give any one particulars respecting her work. She wraps them up in an impenetrable mystery. Like the farmers' wives, who, to our queries, gave no other answer than, " Why, that depends," they take care that no one shall be any the wiser for the questions asked.

The reader may safely follow the directions given in these pages ; not one has been inserted that has not been tested by the writer. To those who are already conversant with bread-making, churning, etc., they may appear needlessly minute ; but we hope the novice may, with very little trouble, become mistress of the subjects to which they refer.

Even if a lady does keep a sufficient number of servants to perform every domestic duty efficiently, still it may prove useful to be able to give instructions to one who may, from some accidental circumstance, be called on to undertake a work to which she has been unaccustomed.

A friend of the writer's, a lady of large fortune, and mistress of a very handsome establishment, said, when speaking of her dairy, " My neighborhood has the character of making very bad butter ; mine is invariably good, and I always get a penny a pound more for it at the 'shop' than my neighbors. If I have occasion to change the dairymaid, and the new one sends me up bad butter, I tell her of it. If it occurs the second time, I make no more complaints ; I go down the next butter-day, and make it entirely myself, having her at my side the whole time. I find I never have to complain again. She sees how it is made, and she is compelled to own it is good. I believe that a servant who is worth keeping will follow any directions, and take any amount of trouble, rather than see 'missus' a second time enter the kitchen or dairy to do her work."

Perhaps the allusion this lady made to the "shop" may puzzle the London reader, but in country places, where more butter is made in a gentleman's family than is required for the consumption of the household, it is sent to—what is frequently—*the* "shop" of the place, and sold for a penny per pound less than the price for which it is retailed by the shopkeeper. The value of the butter is set off against tea, sugar, cheese, and various other articles required in the family in which the butter is made.

When the writer purchased a third cow, it was in anticipation of sending any surplus butter to "shop," and receiving groceries in exchange, nor has she been disappointed.

Every month's additional experience strengthens her conviction of the advantages to be derived from living in the country; and she takes farewell of her readers, in the hope that she has succeeded in conving them that a "farm of four acres" may be made a source of health, profit, and amusement, though many of their "town" friends may threaten them with ruin, should they be rash enough to disregard their advice to take a house in a "nice quiet street," leading into one of the squares.

All the Books on this Catalogue sent by Mail, to any part of the Union, free of postage, upon receipt of Price.

CATALOGUE OF BOOKS
ON
AGRICULTURE AND HORTICULTURE,

PUBLISHED BY
C. M. SAXTON, BARKER & CO.,
No. 25 PARK ROW, NEW YORK.
SUITABLE FOR

SCHOOL, TOWN, AGRICULTURAL, & PRIVATE LIBRARIES.

AMERICAN FARMER'S ENCYCLOPEDIA, - - - - - - $4 00

As a Book of Reference for the Farmer or Gardener, this Work is superior to any other. It contains Reliable Information for the Cultivation of every variety of Field and Garden Crops, the use of all kinds of Manures, descriptions and figures of American insects; and is, indeed, an Agricultural Library in itself, containing *twelve hundred pages*, octavo, and is illustrated by numerous engravings of Grasses, Grains, Animals, Implements, Insects, &c., &c. By GOUVERNEUR EMERSON OF PENNSYLVANIA.

AMERICAN WEEDS AND USEFUL PLANTS, - - - - 1 50

An Illustrated Edition of Agricultural Botany; An Enumeration and Description of Weeds and Useful Plants which merit the notice or require the attention of American Agriculturists. By WM. DARLINGTON, M. D. Revised, with Additions, by GEORGE THURBER, Prof. of Mat. Med. and Botany in the New York College of Pharmacy. Illustrated with nearly 300 Figures, drawn expressly for this work.

ALLEN'S (R. L.) AMERICAN FARM BOOK, - - - - - 1 00

Or a Compend of American Agriculture; being a Practical Treatise on Soils, Manures, Draining, Irrigation, Grasses, Grain, Roots, Fruits, Cotton, Tobacco, Sugar Cane, Rice, and every Staple Product of the United States; with the best methods of Planting, Cultivating and Preparation for Market. Illustrated with more than 100 engravings.

ALLEN'S (R. L.) DISEASES OF DOMESTIC ANIMALS, - - 75

Being a History and Description of the Horse, Mule, Cattle, Sheep, Swine, Poultry and Farm Dogs, with Directions for their Management, Breeding, Crossing, Rearing, Feeding, and Preparation for a Profitable Market; also, their Diseases and Remedies, together with full Directions for the Management of the Dairy, and the comparative Economy and Advantages of Working Animals,—the Horse, Mule, Oxen, &c.

ALLEN'S (L. F.) RURAL ARCHITECTURE, - - - - - 1 25

Being a Complete Description of Farm Houses, Cottages and Out Buildings, comprising Wood Houses, Workshops, Tool Houses, Carriage and Wagon Houses, Stables, Smoke and Ash Houses, Ice Houses, Apiaries or Bee Houses, Poultry Houses, Rabbitry, Dovecote, Piggery, Barns and Sheds for Cattle, &c., &c.; together with Lawns, Pleasure Grounds and Parks; the Flower, Fruit and Vegetable Garden; also, the best method of conducting water into Cattle Yards and Houses. Beautifully illustrated.

ALLEN (J. FISK) ON THE CULTURE OF THE GRAPE, - - 1 00

A Practical Treatise on the Culture and Treatment of the Grape Vine, embracing its History, with Directions for its Treatment in the United States of America, in the Open Air and under Glass Structures, with and without Artificial Heat.

Mailed post paid upon receipt of price.

AMERICAN ARCHITECT, - - - - - - - - - - - 6 00
    COMPRISING ORIGINAL DESIGNS OF CHEAP COUNTRY AND VILLAGE Residences, with Details, Specifications, Plans and Directions, and an Estimate of the Cost of each Design. By JOHN W. RITCH, Architect. First and Second Series, 4to, bound in 1 vol.

AMERICAN FLORIST'S GUIDE, - - - - - - - - 75
    COMPRISING THE AMERICAN ROSE CULTURIST, AND EVERY LADY her own Flower Gardener.

ARRY'S FRUIT GARDEN, - - - - - - - - - - 1 25
    A TREATISE, INTENDED TO EXPLAIN AND ILLUSTRATE THE PHYSIology of Fruit Trees, the Theory and Practice of all Operations connected with the Propagation, Transplanting, Pruning and Training of Orchard and Garden Trees, as Standards, Dwarfs, Pyramids, Espalier, &c. The Laying out and Arranging different kinds of Orchards and Gardens, the selection of suitable varieties for different purposes and localities, Gathering and Preserving Fruits, Treatment of Diseases, Destruction of Insects, Description and Uses of Implements, &c. Illustrated with upwards of 150 Figures. By P. BARRY, of the Mount Hope Nurseries, Rochester, N. Y.

BEMENT'S (C. N.) RABBIT FANCIER, - - - - - - 50
    A TREATISE ON THE BREEDING, REARING, FEEDING AND GENERAL Management of Rabbits, with Remarks upon their Diseases and Remedies, to which are added Full Directions for the Construction of Hutches, Rabbitries, &c., together with Recipes for Cooking and Dressing for the Table. Beautifully illustrated.

BLAKE'S (REV. JOHN L.) FARMER AT HOME, - - - 1 25
    A FAMILY TEXT BOOK FOR THE COUNTRY; being a Cyclopedia of Agricultural Implements and Productions, and of the more important topics in Domestic Economy, Science and Literature, adapted to Rural Life. By Rev. JOHN L. BLAKE, D. D.

BOUSSINGAULT'S (J. B.) RURAL ECONOMY, - - - - 1 25
    OR, CHEMISTRY APPLIED TO AGRICULTURE; PRESENTING DISTINCTLY and in a Simple Manner the Principles of Farm Management, the Preservation and Use of Manures, the Nutrition and Food of Animals, and the General Economy of Agriculture. The work is the fruit of a long life of study and experiment, and its perusal will aid the farmer greatly in obtaining a practical and scientific knowledge of his profession.

BROWNE'S AMERICAN BIRD FANCIER, - - - - - - 25
    THE BREEDING, REARING, FEEDING, MANAGEMENT AND PECULIarities of Cage and House Birds. Illustrated with engravings.

BROWNE'S AMERICAN POULTRY YARD, - - - - - 1 00
    COMPRISING THE ORIGIN, HISTORY AND DESCRIPTION OF THE Different Breeds of Domestic Poultry, with Complete Directions for their Breeding, Crossing, Rearing, Fattening and Preparation for Market; including specific directions for Caponizing Fowls, and for the Treatment of the Principal Diseases to which they are subject, drawn from authentic sources and personal observation. Illustrated with numerous engravings.

BROWNE'S (D. JAY) FIELD BOOK OF MANURES, - - - 1 25
    OR, AMERICAN MUCK BOOK; Treating of the Nature, Properties, Sources, History and Operations of all the Principal Fertilizers and Manures in Common Use, with specific directions for their Preservation and Application to the Soil and to Crops; drawn from authentic sources, actual experience and personal observation, as combined with the Leading Principles of Practical and Scientific Agriculture.

BRIDGEMAN'S (THOS.) YOUNG GARDENER'S ASSISTANT, - - 1 50
    IN THREE PARTS; Containing Catalogues of Garden and Flower Seed, with Practical Directions under each head for the Cultivation of Cu nary Vegetables, Flowers, Fruit Trees, the Grape Vine, &c.; to which is added a Calendar to each part, showing the work necessary to be done in the various departments each month of the year. One volume octavo.

BRIDGEMAN'S KITCHEN GARDENER'S INSTRUCTOR,   ½ Cloth, 50
    "   "   "   "   Cloth, 60

Mailed post paid upon receipt of price.

Books published by C. M. SAXTON, BARKER & CO.

BRIDGEMAN'S FLORIST'S GUIDE, - - - - - - ½ Cloth, 50
" " " - - - - - Cloth, 60
BRIDGEMAN'S FRUIT CULTIVATOR'S MANUAL, - ½ Cloth, 50
" " :" " - - Cloth, 60
BRECK'S BOOK OF FLOWERS, - - - - - - - 1 00
 IN WHICH ARE DESCRIBED ALL THE VARIOUS HARDY HERBACEOUS Perennials, Annuals, Shrubs, Plants and Evergreen Trees, with Directions for their Cultivation.

BUIST'S (ROBERT) AMERICAN FLOWER GARDEN DIRECTORY, 1 25
 CONTAINING PRACTICAL DIRECTIONS FOR THE CULTURE OF PLANTS, in the Flower Garden, Hothouse, Greenhouse, Rooms or Parlor Windows, for every month in the Year ; with a Description of the Plants most desirable in each, the nature of the Soil and situation best adapted to their Growth, the Proper Season for Transplanting, &c. ; with Instructions for erecting a Hothouse, Greenhouse, and Laying out a Flower Garden ; the whole adapted to either Large or Small Gardens, with Instructions for Preparing the Soil, Propagating, Planting, Pruning, Training and Fruiting the Grape Vine.

BUIST'S (ROBERT) FAMILY KITCHEN GARDENER, - - - 75
 CONTAINING PLAIN AND ACCURATE DESCRIPTIONS OF ALL THE Different Species and Varieties of Culinary Vegetables, with their Botanical, English, French and German names, alphabetically arranged, with the Best Mode of Cultivating them in the Garden or under Glass ; also Descriptions and Character of the most Select Fruits, their Management, Propagation, &c. By ROBERT BUIST, author of the "American Flower Garden Directory," &c.

CHINESE SUGAR CANE AND SUGAR-MAKING, - - - - 25
 ITS HISTORY, CULTURE AND ADAPTATION TO THE SOIL, CLIMATE, and Economy of the United States, with an Account of Various Processes of Manufacturing Sugar. Drawn from authentic sources, by CHARLES F. STANSBURY, A. M., late Commissioner at the Exhibition of all Nations at London.

CHORLTON'S GRAPE-GROWER'S GUIDE, - - - - - 60
 INTENDED ESPECIALLY FOR THE AMERICAN CLIMATE. Being a Practical Treatise on the Cultivation of the Grape Vine in each department of Hothouse, Cold Grapery, Retarding House and Out-door Culture. With Plans for the construction of the Requisite Buildings, and giving the best methods for Heating the same. Every department being fully illustrated. By WILLIAM CHORLTON.

COBBETT'S AMERICAN GARDENER, - - - - - - 50
 A TREATISE ON THE SITUATION, SOIL AND LAYING-OUT OF GARDENS, and the Making and Managing of Hotbeds and Greenhouses, and on the Propagation and Cultivation of the several sorts of Vegetables, Herbs, Fruits and Flowers.

COTTAGE AND FARM BEE-KEEPER, - - - - - - 50
 A PRACTICAL WORK, by a Country Curate.

COLE'S AMERICAN FRUIT BOOK, - - - - - - - 50
 CONTAINING DIRECTIONS FOR RAISING, PROPAGATING AND MANAGing Fruit Trees, Shrubs and Plants ; with a Description of the Best Varieties of Fruit, including New and Valuable Kinds.

COLE'S AMERICAN VETERINARIAN, - - - - - - 50
 CONTAINING DISEASES OF DOMESTIC ANIMALS, THEIR CAUSES, Symptoms and Remedies ; with Rules for Restoring and Preserving Health by good management ; also for Training and Breeding.

DADD'S AMERICAN CATTLE DOCTOR, - - - - - - 1 00
 CONTAINING THE NECESSARY INFORMATION FOR PRESERVING THE Health and Curing the Diseases of Oxen, Cows, Sheep and Swine, with a Great Variety of Original Recipes and Valuable Information in reference to Farm and Dairy Management, whereby every Man can be his own Cattle Doctor. The principles taught in this work are, that all Medication shall be subservient to Nature—that all Medicines must be sanative in their operation, and administered with a view of aiding the vital powers, instead of depressing, as heretofore, with the lancet or by poison. By G. H. DADD, M. D. Veterinary practitioner.

Mailed post paid upon receipt of price.

DADD'S MODERN HORSE DOCTOR, - - - - - - - 1 00
    AN AMERICAN BOOK FOR AMERICAN FARMERS; Containing Practical Observations on the Causes, Nature and Treatment of Disease and Lameness of Horses, embracing the Most Recent and Approved Methods, according to an enlightened system of Veterinary Practice, for the Preservation and Restoration of Health. With illustrations.

DADD'S ANATOMY AND PHYSIOLOGY OF THE HORSE, Plain, - 2 00
    "   "   "   "   " Colored Plates, 4 00
    WITH ANATOMICAL AND QUESTIONAL ILLUSTRATIONS; Containing, also, a Series of Examinations on Equine Anatomy and Philosophy, with Instructions in reference to Dissection and the mode of making Anatomical Preparations; to which is added a Glossary of Veterinary Technicalities, Toxicological Chart, and Dictionary of Veterinary Science.

DANA'S MUCK MANUAL, FOR THE USE OF FARMERS, - - 1 00
    A TREATISE ON THE PHYSICAL AND CHEMICAL PROPERTIES OF SOILS and Chemistry of Manures; including, also, the subject of Composts, Artificial Manures and Irrigation. A new edition, with a Chapter on Bones and Superphosphates.

DANA'S PRIZE ESSAY ON MANURES, - - - - - - - 25
    SUBMITTED TO THE TRUSTEES OF THE MASSACHUSETTS SOCIETY FOR Promoting Agriculture, for their Premium. By SAMUEL H. DANA.

DOMESTIC AND ORNAMENTAL POULTRY, Plain Plates, - - 1 00
    "   "   " Colored Plates, - - 2 00
    A TREATISE ON THE HISTORY AND MANAGEMENT OF ORNAMENTAL and Domestic Poultry. By Rev. EDMUND SAUL DIXON, A. M., with large additions by J. J. KERR, M. D. Illustrated with sixty-five Original Portraits, engraved expressly for this work. Fourth edition, revised.

DOWNING'S (A. J.) LANDSCAPE GARDENING, - - - - 3 50
    REVISED, ENLARGED AND NEWLY ILLUSTRATED, BY HENRY WINthrop Sargent. This Great Work, which has accomplished so much in elevating the American Taste for Rural Improvements, is now rendered doubly interesting and valuable by the experience of all the Prominent Cultivators of Ornamental Trees in the United States, and by the descriptions of American Places, Private Residences, Central Park, New York, Llewellyn Park, New Jersey, and a full account of the Newer Deciduous and Evergreen Trees and Shrubs. The illustrations of this edition consist of *seven superb steel plate engravings*, by SMILLIE, HINSHELWOOD, DUTHIE and others; besides *one hundred engravings on wood and stone*, of the best American Residences and Parks, with Portraits of many New or Remarkable Trees and Shrubs.

DOWNING'S (A. J.) RURAL ESSAYS, - - - - - - - 3 00
    ON HORTICULTURE, LANDSCAPE GARDENING, RURAL ARCHITECTURE, Trees, Agriculture, Fruit, with his Letters from England. Edited, with a Memoir of the Author, by GEORGE WM. CURTIS, and a Letter to his Friends, by FREDERIKA BREMER, and an elegant Steel Portrait of the Author.

EASTWOOD (B.) ON THE CULTIVATION OF THE CRANBERRY, 50
    WITH A DESCRIPTION OF THE BEST VARIETIES. By B. EASTWOOD, "Septimus," of the New York Tribune. Illustrated.

ELLIOTT'S WESTERN FRUIT BOOK, - - - - - - - 1 25
    A NEW EDITION OF THIS WORK, THOROUGHLY REVISED. Embracing all the New and Valuable Fruits, with the Latest Improvements in their Cultivation, up to January, 1859. especially adapted to the wants of Western Fruit Growers; full of excellent illustrations. By F. R. ELLIOTT, Pomologist, late of Cleveland, Ohio, now of St. Louis.

EVERY LADY HER OWN FLOWER GARDENER, - - - - 50
    ADDRESSED TO THE INDUSTRIOUS AND ECONOMICAL ONLY; containing simple and practical Directions for Cultivating Plants and Flowers; also, Hints for the Management of Flowers in Rooms, with brief Botanical Descriptions of Plants and Flowers. The whole in plain and simple language. By LOUISA JOHNSON.

Mailed post paid upon receipt of price.

Books published by C. M. SAXTON, BARKER & Co. 5

FARM DRAINAGE, - - - - - - - - - - 1 00
    THE PRINCIPLES, PROCESSES AND EFFECTS OF DRAINING LAND, with Stones, Wood, Drain-plows, Open Ditches, and especially with Tiles; including Tables of Rainfall, Evaporation, Filtration, Excavation, capacity of Pipes, cost and number to the acre. With more than 100 illustrations. By the Hon. HENRY F. FRENCH, of New Hampshire.

FESSENDEN'S (T. G.) AMERICAN KITCHEN GARDENER, - - 50
    CONTAINING DIRECTIONS FOR THE CULTIVATION OF VEGETABLES AND Garden Fruits. Cloth.

FESSENDEN'S COMPLETE FARMER AND AMERICAN GARDENER, 1 25
    RURAL ECONOMIST AND NEW AMERICAN GARDENER; Containing a Compendious Epitome of the most Important Branches of Agriculture and Rural Economy; with Practical Directions on the Cultivation of Fruits and Vegetables, including Landscape and Ornamental Gardening. By THOMAS G. FESSENDEN. 2 vols. in 1.

FIELD'S PEAR CULTURE, - - - - - - - - - 1 00
    THE PEAR GARDEN; or, a Treatise on the Propagation and Cultivation of the Pear Tree, with Instructions for its Management from the Seedling to the Bearing Tree. By THOMAS W. FIELD.

FISH CULTURE, - - - - - - - - - - - 1 00
    A TREATISE ON THE ARTIFICIAL PROPAGATION OF FISH, AND THE Construction of Ponds, with the Description and Habits of such kinds of Fish as are most suitable for Pisciculture. By THEODATUS GARLICK, M. D., Vice-President of the Cleveland Academy of Nat. Science.

FLINT ON GRASSES, - - - - - - - - - - 1 25
    A PRACTICAL TREATISE ON GRASSES AND FORAGE PLANTS; Comprising their Natural History, Comparative Nutritive Value, Methods of Cultivation, Cutting, Curing and the Management of Grass Lands. By CHARLES L. FLINT, A. M., Secretary of the Mass. State Board of Agriculture.

GUENON ON MILCH COWS, - - - - - - - - 60
    A TREATISE ON MILCH COWS, whereby the Quality and Quantity of Milk which any Cow will give may be accurately determined by observing Natural Marks or External Indications alone; the length of time she will continue to give Milk, &c., &c. By M. FRANCIS GUENON, of Libourne, France. Translated by NICHOLAS P. TRIST, Esq.; with Introduction, Remarks and Observations on the Cow and the Dairy, by JOHN S. SKINNER. Illustrated with numerous Engravings. Neatly done up in paper covers, 37 cts.

HERBERT'S HINTS TO HORSE-KEEPERS, - - - - - 1 25
    COMPLETE MANUAL FOR HORSEMEN; Embracing:
    HOW TO BREED A HORSE.   HOW TO PHYSIC A HORSE.
    HOW TO BUY A HORSE.   (ALLOPATHY AND HOMŒOPATHY
    HOW TO BREAK A HORSE.   HOW TO GROOM A HORSE.
    HOW TO USE A HORSE.   HOW TO DRIVE A HORSE.
    HOW TO FEED A HORSE.   HOW TO RIDE A HORSE.
And Chapters on Mules and Ponies. By the late HENRY WILLIAM HERBERT (FRANK FORRESTER); with additions, including RAREY'S METHOD OF HORSE TAMING, and BAUCHER'S SYSTEM OF HORSEMANSHIP; also, giving directions for the Selection and Care of Carriages and Harness of every description, from the City "Turn Out" to the Farmer's "Gear," and a Biography of the eccentric Author. *Illustrated throughout.*

HOOPER'S DOG AND GUN, - - - - - - - - 50
    A FEW LOOSE CHAPTERS ON SHOOTING, among which will be found some Anecdotes and Incidents; also Instructions for Dog Breaking, and interesting letters from Sportsmen. By A BAD SHOT.

HYDE'S CHINESE SUGAR CANE, - - - - - - - 25
    CONTAINING ITS HISTORY, MODE OF CULTURE, MANUFACTURE OF the Sugar, &c.; with Reports of its success in different parts of the United States.

Mailed post paid upon receipt of price.

Books published by C. M. SAXTON, BARKER & Co.

JOHNSTON'S (JAMES F. W.) AGRICULTURAL CHEMISTRY, - 1 25
LECTURES ON THE APPLICATION OF CHEMISTRY AND GEOLOGY TO Agriculture. New Edition, with an Appendix, containing the Author's Experiments in Practical Agriculture.

JOHNSTON'S (J F. W.) ELEMENTS OF AGRICULTURAL CHEMISTRY AND GEOLOGY, - - - - - - - - 1 00
WITH A COMPLETE ANALYTICAL AND ALPHABETICAL INDEX, and an American Preface. By Hon. SIMON BROWN, Editor of the "New England Farmer."

OHNSTON'S (J. F. W.) CATECHISM OF AGRICULTURAL CHEMISTRY AND GEOLOGY, - - - - - - - - 25
By JAMES F. W. JOHNSTON, Honorary Member of the Royal Agricultural Society of England, and author of "Lectures on Agricultural Chemistry and Geology." With an Introduction by JOHN PITKIN NORTON, M. A., late Professor of Scientific Agriculture in Yale College. With Notes and Additions by the Author, prepared expressly for this edition, and an Appendix compiled by the Superintendent of Education in Nova Scotia. Adapted to the use of Schools.

LANGSTROTH (REV. L. L.) ON THE HIVE AND HONEY BEE, - 1 25
A PRACTICAL TREATISE ON THE HIVE AND HONEY BEE, Third edition, enlarged and *illustrated with numerous engravings*. This Work is, without a doubt, the best work on the Bee published in any language, whether we consider its scientific accuracy, the practical instructions it contains, or the beauty and completeness of its illustrations.

LEUCHARS' HOW TO BUILD AND VENTILATE HOTHOUSES, - 1 25
A PRACTICAL TREATISE ON THE CONSTRUCTION, HEATING AND Ventilation of Hothouses, including Conservatories, Greenhouses, Graperies and other kinds of Horticultural Structures; with Practical Directions for their Management, in regard to Light, Heat and Air. Illustrated with numerous engravings. By P. B. LEUCHARS, Garden Architect.

LIEBIG'S (JUSTUS) FAMILIAR LECTURES ON CHEMISTRY, - 50
AND ITS RELATION TO COMMERCE, PHYSIOLOGY, and AGRICULTURE. Edited by JOHN GARDENER, M. D.,

LINSLEY'S MORGAN HORSES, - - - - - - - - 1 00
A PREMIUM ESSAY ON THE ORIGIN, HISTORY, AND CHARACTERISTICS of this remarkable American Breed of Horses; tracing the Pedigree from the original Justin Morgan, through the most noted of his progeny, down to the present time. With numerous portraits. To which are added Hints for Breeding, Breaking and General Use and Management of Horses, with practical Directions for Training them for Exhibition at Agricultural Fairs. By D. C. LINSLEY, Editor of the American Stock Journal.

MOORE'S RURAL HAND BOOKS, - - - - - - - - 1 25
FIRST SERIES, containing Treatises on—
THE HORSE,   THE PESTS OF THE FARM,
THE HOG,   DOMESTIC FOWLS, and
THE HONEY BEE,   THE COW.

SECOND SERIES, containing—   - - -   1 25
EVERY LADY HER OWN FLOWER GARDENER,   ESSAY ON MANURES,
ELEMENTS OF AGRICULTURE,   AMERICAN KITCHEN GARDENER,
BIRD FANCIER,   AMERICAN ROSE CULTURIST.

THIRD SERIES, containing—   - - - -   1 25
MILES ON THE HORSE'S FOOT,   VINE-DRESSER'S MANUAL,
THE RABBIT FANCIER,   BEE-KEEPER'S CHART,
WEEKS ON BEES,   CHEMISTRY MADE EASY.

FOURTH SERIES, containing—   - - - -   1 25
PERSOZ ON THE VINE,   HOOPER'S DOG AND GUN,
LIEBIG'S FAMILIAR LETTERS,   SKILLFUL HOUSEWIFE,
            BROWNE'S MEMOIRS OF INDIAN CORN.

Mailed post paid upon receipt of price.

www.ingramcontent.com/pod-product-compliance
Lightning Source LLC
Chambersburg PA
CBHW020106170426
43199CB00009B/416